A Year of Loving God
52 Bible Inspired Lessons and Practices Weekly Workbook

Copyright © 2025 by Magdalena Szopa
All rights reserved. No part of this book may be reproduced, stored in a retrieval system, or transmitted in any form or by any means, electronic or mechanical, including photocopying, recording, or by any information storage and retrieval system, without written permission from the publisher, except for brief quotations in reviews or scholarly articles.
Published by Compassionate Living Books LLC

www.CompassionateLivingBooks.com
ISBN: **979-8-90046-182-3**
First edition
Printed in the United States of America

Unless otherwise indicated, Scripture quotations are from the King James Version which is in the public domain.

This workbook is intended for personal spiritual growth. It is not a substitute for professional counseling, medical, or legal advice. Use discretion and seek appropriate help when needed.

A YEAR OF LOVING GOD

52 Bible Inspired Lessons and Practices

Weekly Workbook

By Magdalena Szopa

www.CompassionateLivingBooks.com

Before You Begin 7

Introduction. A Year of Loving God 8

Week 1. Wholehearted love and devotion 10

Week 2. Trust and faith 15

Week 3. Obedience that flows from love 20

Week 4. Worship in spirit and truth 25

Week 5. Singing and musical praise 30

Week 6. Prayer that asks and trusts 35

Week 7. Listening to Scripture with mind and heart 40

Week 8. Repentance and confession 46

Week 9. Gratitude and thanksgiving 51

Week 10. Forgiveness given and received 56

Week 11. Mercy and simple service 61

Week 12. Integrity and truthful speech 66

Week 13. Patience and long suffering 71

Week 14. Waiting on the Lord with hope 76

Week 15. Simplicity and freedom from idols 81

Week 16. Contentment without greed 86

Week 17. Purity of heart and mind 91

Week 18. Stewardship of time and resources 96

Week 19. Blessing enemies and refusing revenge 101

Week 20. Quick to listen and slow to speak 106

Week 21. Just and fair work and money 111

Week 22. Encouragement that builds others up 116

Week 23. Refusing grumbling and gossip 121

Week 24. Intercession for others in prayer 126

Week 25. Cheerful giving and first steps in generosity 131

Week 26. Integrity in secret places 136

Week 27. Perseverance in prayer and good works 141

Week 28. Daily cross bearing and following Jesus 146

Week 29. Seeking refuge in God rather than in power 151

Week 30. Righteous anger without sin 156

Week 31. Care for creation as God's world 160

Week 32. Impartiality and equal dignity for all 165

Week 33. Creative beauty offered as worship 170

Week 34. Excellence and diligence in our work 175

Week 35. Honesty in speech and promise keeping 179

Week 36. Hospitality to strangers and friends 184

Week 37. Using gifts to serve others 189

Week 38. Unity and keeping the bond of peace 194

Week 39. Humble submission to rightful authority 199

Week 40. Courage to speak truth in love 203

Week 41. Bearing with one another in patience 208

Week 42. Gentleness and meek strength 213

Week 43. Self control in body and mind 218

Week 44. Teaching children the way of the Lord 223

Week 45. Remembering the poor 229

Week 46. Visiting the sick and the imprisoned 234

Week 47. Caring for widows and orphans 239

Week 48. Courageous witness to the good news 244

Week 49. Sexual purity and honor 249

Week 50. Hiding the word in your heart 254

Week 51. Lament and hope in sorrow 259

Week 52. Living sacrifice and a renewed mind 264

Afterword. Keep Walking in Love 269

Before You Begin

This book is for anyone who wants to learn how to love God in real life. It works whether you are brand new to the Bible or you have read it for years. It also works if you are exploring faith on your own. You do not need a group, a class, or a programs or routines at home to use these pages. Come as you are. Bring an honest heart and a willingness to practice small steps.

The Bible leads the way. Each week you will read a short passage in the King James Version, see what the verses say, and learn simple ways to practice them in daily life. The goal is not to collect information. The goal is to let God's word shape your thoughts, choices, and habits so that love grows.

Set yourself up to succeed. Choose a quiet place, a simple time, and a small plan. Five to fifteen minutes can be enough to begin. Keep a pen and a notebook nearby. Read the verses slowly. Notice a word or a line that stands out. Ask, What does this show me about God. Ask, What is one small step I can take today.

Go week by week. You do not have to do everything at once. Take the next step you can see. Some weeks will feel natural. Others will stretch you. That is normal. When you stumble, start again. God is patient and kind. He loves steady beginners.

Keep it practical. These pages name choices you can make with your time, your words, your money, and your attention. They fit busy days. They can be done in a kitchen, on a lunch break, in a parked car, or at a bedside. Small seeds planted often will grow.

Let grace lead you. You are not trying to earn God's love. You are answering the love he has already shown in Jesus Christ. Every yes you give is a response to mercy. Trust him to meet you as you practice. Ask for help. Thank him for any progress. Begin again tomorrow.

Introduction. A Year of Loving God

You were made for love. From the first pages of Scripture to the last, the story is God drawing near to people and people learning to answer him with trust, joy, and obedience. Jesus said the greatest commandment is to love the Lord your God with all your heart, soul, mind, and strength. This book is an invitation to practice that love in daily life. It is beginner friendly. You do not need background knowledge, programs or routines at home, or special tools. You need a Bible, a little quiet, and a willing heart.

In the Bible, love is more than a feeling. Love is a lived response to the God who first loved us. It shows up in choices, habits, and words. It orders our desires and clears our vision. When love leads, obedience becomes possible and beautiful. These pages are built to help you live that kind of love with simple, steady steps. You will read a short passage in the King James Version, see what the verses say, and learn how to practice them in your ordinary world.

This book is arranged for one year of weekly lessons. There are fifty two weeks that each focus on one way to love God according to Scripture. Think of them as facets of a single jewel. Each facet catches the light from a different angle, but it is all one love for one Lord. Some weeks will feel familiar. Others may stretch you. That is normal. Take the next small step you can see. God meets beginners with patience and power.

The pattern is simple. First, read the passage slowly. Second, notice what the verses say. Third, act on one clear practice. Do not worry about doing everything. Do something true today. Small seeds, sown often, become a harvest. When you stumble, begin again. When the heart feels cold, show up anyway and ask for help. As you obey in little ways, love deepens and joy grows.

You will also find help for hard places. Scripture gives language for grief, courage for waiting, and wisdom for conflict. It teaches forgiveness and truth telling, generosity and purity, prayer and trust. These are not ideas to admire from a distance. They are everyday choices in calendars, budgets, and conversations. As you take them up one by one, you will notice God at work in you and through you.

A few encouragements as you start your year. Start where you are. If one week meets you in this season, begin there. Keep it simple and steady. Five to fifteen minutes is enough to begin. Let grace lead. You are not trying to earn God's love. You are answering the love he has already shown in Jesus Christ. When you fail, confess and start again. When you see even a small change, give thanks.

If you wonder whether these ways truly matter, remember how Jesus sees secret faithfulness. He notices a quiet prayer, an honest word, a hidden act of mercy, a patient choice to forgive. He receives every small yes and multiplies it. None of it is lost on him. So open your Bible, open your heart, and walk one week at a time. May God take every small yes and shape it into an answer worthy of his great love.

Week 1. Wholehearted love and devotion

Focus

Love God first with all that you are, and let that love order everything else.

Deuteronomy 6:5 (KJV)

"And thou shalt love the LORD thy God with all thine heart, and with all thy soul, and with all thy might."

Matthew 22:37 (KJV)

"Jesus said unto him, Thou shalt love the Lord thy God with all thy heart, and with all thy soul, and with all thy mind."

What the verses say

Deuteronomy speaks to the whole person. Heart is the center of desire and decision. Soul is your very life. Might includes your strength, energy, and resources. Jesus adds mind, showing that love for God is thoughtful and alert. These commands describe a single love expressed through every part of you.

Wholehearted does not mean you never feel weak. It means God is first. When other good things try to take the top place, this command calls you back. From this center, everything else finds order. Love becomes the root that feeds obedience, honesty, generosity, and compassion.

This love is covenant loyalty. It is more than a temporary emotion. You return to God after wandering. You set your face toward him again and again. You choose what helps love grow and you turn from what drains it.

Scripture puts love before achievement. God wants your heart. The practices in this book help your heart stay pointed toward him in ordinary life.

How to practice this on your own

Give God your first minutes. Sit down, breathe slowly, and read a few verses. Speak to him with simple words. "Father, I am here. Teach me to love you today." Keep a short prayer close to use through the day.

Shape your inputs. Choose one media fast that helps love grow. For one week reduce what distracts or inflames envy. Use the saved minutes to read a psalm or to be quiet before God.

Write a small rule of love. One line for morning, one for midday, one for evening. Example. Morning. Read and pray for five minutes. Midday. Pause to thank God for one gift. Evening. Review the day and confess what needs mercy. Keep it very small so you can keep it.

Let love lead your choices. If an option weakens love, set it aside. If an option strengthens love, choose it. This can touch money, screens, relationships, and work habits. Start with one area and make one change you can keep.

End each day with return. Ask, Where did love lead me today and where did I wander. Thank God for any step forward. Ask for mercy where you failed. Rest in his care and begin again tomorrow.

Reflect and Practice

Key Scriptures to copy by hand

Write one or both verses on the lines below.

_____

_____

_____

1) What did God show me as I read this week

_____

_____

_____

_____

2) Where is my love for God strong right now

_____

_____

_____

_____

3) Where is my love divided or distracted

_____

_____

_____

_____

4) One obstacle that keeps me from loving God with all my heart

_____

_____

_____

_____

5) One concrete step I will take this week

Example: Set time for prayer, a verse to carry, a choice I will make for God first.

_____

_____

_____

_____

6) My simple rule of life for this week

Morning.
_____

Midday.
_____

Evening.
_____

7) Scripture to memorize

Write the verse and keep it with you.

_____

_____

_____

_____

8) Gratitude to warm my love for God

List three gifts from the last day.

1. _____

_____

2. _____

_____

3. _____

_____

9) Love in action

Who will I serve or encourage because I love God?

Name.

_____

Plan.

_____

_____

10) Prayer of offering

Write a short prayer to give God first place.

_____

_____

_____

_____

11) Talk with someone

Whom will I tell about my step this week?

Name.

_____

When we will talk.

_____?

12) End of week examen

Where did I love God with all my heart this week?

_____

_____

Where did I resist and what will I do next?

_____

_____

What help do I need from God and from others?

_____

_____

Week 2. Trust and faith

Focus

Trust the Lord with all your heart and walk by faith in daily decisions.

Proverbs 3:5 to 6 (KJV)

"Trust in the LORD with all thine heart; and lean not unto thine own understanding. In all thy ways acknowledge him, and he shall direct thy paths."

Hebrews 11:1 (KJV)

"Now faith is the substance of things hoped for, the evidence of things not seen."

What the verses say

Trust rests on God's character. To lean on your own understanding means to treat your analysis as final. Scripture does not forbid thinking.

It warns against trusting your thoughts more than you trust God. To acknowledge him is to bring him into the center of your ways and to submit to his wisdom.

Faith has substance and evidence. It is not blind. It stands on what God has said and done. You may not see every step, but you can walk with confidence in the light you have. As you trust him, he makes the path straight enough for your next step.

Trust and action belong together. You pray and you work. You ask and you move. Faith does not wait for perfect certainty. It obeys the truth already known and leaves the rest to God.

How to practice this on your own

Begin with a trust list. Write three truths about God from Scripture. Example. God is faithful. God gives wisdom. God cares for me. Place the list where you see it. Read it when anxiety rises.

Use a simple decision sheet. Name the decision. List options. Note which options align with Scripture and which conflict. Cross out what conflicts. Pray Psalm 25. Then choose the best remaining option you can see and take one small step.

Practice a worry exchange. When fear loops in your mind, replace the story with one promise. Say it aloud. Then do one right action that fits the promise. Over time this trains the heart to lean on God rather than on fear.

Keep a record of God's help. Date a page. Write one sentence about an answered prayer or a quiet strength you received. Return to this when trust feels thin. Memory feeds faith.

Reflect and Practice

Key Scriptures to copy by hand

Write one or both verses on the lines below.

_____

_____

_____

_____

1) What did God show me as I read this week

_____

_____

_____

_____

2) Where is my love for God strong right now

_____

_____

_____

_____

3) Where is my love divided or distracted

_____

_____

_____

_____

4) One obstacle that keeps me from loving God with all my heart

_____

_____

_____

_____

5) One concrete step I will take this week

Example: Set time for prayer, a verse to carry, a choice I will make for God first.

_____

_____

_____

_____

6) My simple rule of life for this week

Morning.
_____

Midday.
_____

Evening.
_____

7) Scripture to memorize

Write the verse and keep it with you.

_____

_____

_____

_____

8) Gratitude to warm my love for God

List three gifts from the last day.

1. _____

_____

2. _____

_____

3. _____

_____

9) Love in action

Who will I serve or encourage because I love God?

Name.
_____

Plan.
_____

_____

10) Prayer of offering

Write a short prayer to give God first place.

_____

_____

_____

_____

11) Talk with someone

Whom will I tell about my step this week?

Name.
_____

When we will talk.
_____?

12) End of week examen

Where did I love God with all my heart this week?
_____
_____

Where did I resist and what will I do next?
_____
_____

What help do I need from God and from others?
_____
_____

Week 3. Obedience that flows from love

Focus

Keep Christ's commandments gladly, not to earn love but because you are loved.

John 14:15 (KJV)

"If ye love me, keep my commandments."

1 John 5:3 (KJV)

"For this is the love of God, that we keep his commandments: and his commandments are not grievous."

What the verses say

Love leads and obedience follows. God's commands are not cruel. They fit how he made you and they protect life. Obedience becomes freedom because it breaks the grip of lies and disorder.

When you fail, you are not finished. Confession returns you to the Father. You repair what you can and start again. Love grows stronger as you practice obedience under mercy?

Obedience is concrete. It appears in speech that tells the truth, in promises kept, in boundaries that honor purity, in generosity that trusts God to provide, and in mercy that refuses revenge.

How to practice this on your own

Make one pre decision in a weak area. Decide now what you will do before the pressure arrives. Example. When I am angry, I will pause for one minute and pray before I reply. Write your pre decision on a card and keep it near.

Stack a holy habit onto a daily habit. After I make coffee, I will read one paragraph of Scripture. After I lock the door, I will thank God for one gift. Habit stacking makes obedience easier to start and easier to keep.

Use clear boundaries with screens. Move the phone out of the bedroom. Set a last screen time. Use filters or settings that help you choose purity. Boundaries are not fear. They are wisdom for love.

End the day with confession and gratitude. Speak plainly to God about where you strayed. Receive forgiveness and plan one small repair if needed. Thank him for any obedience he helped you offer.

Reflect and Practice

Key Scriptures to copy by hand

Write one or both verses on the lines below.

_____

_____

_____

_____

1) What did God show me as I read this week

_____

_____

_____

_____

2) Where is my love for God strong right now

_____

_____

_____

_____

3) Where is my love divided or distracted

_____

_____

_____

_____

4) One obstacle that keeps me from loving God with all my heart

_____

_____

_____

_____

5) One concrete step I will take this week

Example: Set time for prayer, a verse to carry, a choice I will make for God first.

_____

_____

_____

_____

6) My simple rule of life for this week

Morning.
_____

Midday.
_____

Evening.
_____

7) Scripture to memorize

Write the verse and keep it with you.

_____

_____

_____

8) Gratitude to warm my love for God

List three gifts from the last day.

1. _____

2. _____

3. _____

9) Love in action

Who will I serve or encourage because I love God?

Name.
_____

Plan.
_____

10) Prayer of offering

Write a short prayer to give God first place.

_____

_____

_____

_____

11) Talk with someone

Whom will I tell about my step this week?

Name.
_____

When we will talk.
_____?

12) End of week examen

Where did I love God with all my heart this week?
_____
_____

Where did I resist and what will I do next?
_____
_____

What help do I need from God and from others?
_____
_____

Week 4. Worship in spirit and truth

Focus

Draw near to God with a sincere heart, shaped by Scripture and filled with the Spirit.

John 4:23 to 24 (KJV)

"But the hour cometh, and now is, when the true worshippers shall worship the Father in spirit and in truth: for the Father seeketh such to worship him. God is a Spirit: and they that worship him must worship him in spirit and in truth."

Psalm 95:6 (KJV)

"O come, let us worship and bow down: let us kneel before the LORD our maker."

What the verses say

God seeks worship that is real inside and aligned with truth. Spirit means more than a feeling. It means sincerity before God. Truth means worship that matches what God has revealed in Scripture and in Christ.

Bowing is an honest response to a great God. Worship involves mind, heart, and body. It is not entertainment. It is meeting with the living God who made you and loves you.

Personal worship does not need special equipment. A chair, a Bible, and a willing heart are enough. The goal is not to perform. The goal is to be present to God with love and truth.

How to practice this on your own

Create a simple place. Keep your Bible, a pen, and a small notebook together. Light a candle if it helps you focus. Begin with one minute of silence.

Read a psalm aloud each day this week. Let the words set the tone. Pause on a line that speaks to you. Answer God with your own words.

Add a physical act. Kneel for a short prayer or open your hands as a sign of trust. Small bodily acts help the heart pay attention.

Carry worship into ordinary work. Before a task say, "Lord, I offer this to you." Do it with honesty and care. This turns daily work into quiet worship.

When worship feels dry, keep showing up. Tell God the truth about how you feel. Ask for fresh help. Often joy returns as you persist with simple faithfulness?

Reflect and Practice

Key Scriptures to copy by hand

Write one or both verses on the lines below.

_____

_____

_____

_____

1) What did God show me as I read this week

_____

_____

_____

_____

2) Where is my love for God strong right now

_____

_____

_____

_____

3) Where is my love divided or distracted

_____

_____

_____

_____

4) One obstacle that keeps me from loving God with all my heart

_____

_____

_____

_____

5) One concrete step I will take this week

Example: Set time for prayer, a verse to carry, a choice I will make for God first.

_____

_____

_____

_____

6) My simple rule of life for this week

Morning.
_____

Midday.
_____

Evening.
_____

7) Scripture to memorize

Write the verse and keep it with you.

_____

_____

_____

_____

8) Gratitude to warm my love for God

List three gifts from the last day.

1. _____

   _____

2. _____

   _____

3. _____

   _____

9) Love in action

Who will I serve or encourage because I love God?

Name.

_____

Plan.

_____

_____

10) Prayer of offering

Write a short prayer to give God first place.

_____

_____

_____

11) Talk with someone

Whom will I tell about my step this week?

Name.
_____

When we will talk.
_____?

12) End of week examen

Where did I love God with all my heart this week?
_____
_____

Where did I resist and what will I do next?
_____
_____

What help do I need from God and from others?
_____
_____

Week 5. Singing and musical praise

Focus

Lift your voice to God with Scripture shaped songs where you live.

Psalm 96:1 (KJV)

"O sing unto the LORD a new song: sing unto the LORD, all the earth."

Ephesians 5:19 (KJV)

"Speaking to yourselves in psalms and hymns and spiritual songs, singing and making melody in your heart to the Lord."

What the verses say

God invites everyone to sing. New songs rise because his mercies are new. Songs carry Scripture into memory and plant truth in the heart. They help us rejoice, grieve, and hope before God.

The heart's melody matters. God receives sincere praise in any voice. Whispered song in a kitchen is as precious as skill on a stage when it is offered in love.

How to practice this on your own

Build a small Scripture song list. Choose a few hymns and choruses that quote or closely echo the Bible. Keep the list in your phone. Sing one each morning or evening.

Include songs of lament and hope. Life holds sorrow. Give it honest words. Sing a psalm of lament followed by a song of trust. This trains your heart to bring pain and hope to God together.

If you play an instrument, practice as an offering. Before you begin say, "Lord, receive this." If you do not play, hum or sing softly. God delights in sincere praise.

Use song to teach children or to steady your own heart. A short chorus can calm fear and lift the mind to God in a few seconds.

Reflect and Practice

Key Scriptures to copy by hand

Write one or both verses on the lines below.

_____

_____

_____

_____

1) What did God show me as I read this week

_____

_____

_____

_____

2) Where is my love for God strong right now

_____

_____

_____

_____

3) Where is my love divided or distracted

_____

_____

_____

_____

4) One obstacle that keeps me from loving God with all my heart

_____

_____

_____

_____

5) One concrete step I will take this week

Example: Set time for prayer, a verse to carry, a choice I will make for God first.

_____

_____

_____

_____

6) My simple rule of life for this week

Morning.
_____

Midday.
_____

Evening.
_____

7) Scripture to memorize

Write the verse and keep it with you.

_____

_____

_____

_____

8) Gratitude to warm my love for God

List three gifts from the last day.

1. _____

_____

2. _____

_____

3. _____

_____

9) Love in action

Who will I serve or encourage because I love God?

Name.

_____

Plan.

_____

_____

10) Prayer of offering

Write a short prayer to give God first place.

_____

_____

_____

_____

11) Talk with someone

Whom will I tell about my step this week?

Name.

_____

When we will talk.

_____?

12) End of week examen

Where did I love God with all my heart this week?

_____

_____

Where did I resist and what will I do next?

_____

_____

What help do I need from God and from others?

_____

_____

Week 6. Prayer that asks and trusts

Focus

Bring everything to God in prayer with honest requests and quiet trust.

Philippians 4:6 to 7 (KJV)

"Be careful for nothing; but in every thing by prayer and supplication with thanksgiving let your requests be made known unto God. And the peace of God, which passeth all understanding, shall keep your hearts and minds through Christ Jesus."

Matthew 7:7 to 8 (KJV)

"Ask, and it shall be given you; seek, and ye shall find; knock, and it shall be opened unto you: For every one that asketh receiveth; and he that seeketh findeth; and to him that knocketh it shall be opened."

What the verses say

Scripture invites you to bring every concern to God. Thanksgiving belongs in every request. Gratitude keeps the heart soft while you ask. The promise is peace that stands guard over your heart and mind in Christ.

Jesus teaches persistence. Ask, seek, and knock are active words. You keep praying because you trust the Father's care. Prayer is not a machine that guarantees outcomes. It is a relationship of trust with the God who knows you.

As you pray, you will notice answers. Some are yes. Some are no. Many are wait. In each case God is near and at work.

How to practice this on your own

Keep a simple prayer rhythm. Morning. Thank God for three gifts and ask for help with three tasks. Midday. Pray one verse and one sentence for someone else. Evening. Review the day, confess any sin, and thank God for one mercy.

Use Scripture as language for prayer. Read a psalm line by line and answer each line in your own words. This keeps prayer honest and anchored.

Create a small list for intercession. Write five names. Pray for one or two each day. Add a single practical good you can do for them this week.

When worry surges, stop and pray a short prayer. "Lord, have mercy." "Father, help me." Then take one right action you already know to do?

Keep an answered prayers page. Date it. Write one sentence. Return to it often. This builds confidence to keep asking and to keep trusting.

Reflect and Practice

Key Scriptures to copy by hand

Write one or both verses on the lines below.

_____

_____

_____

_____

1) What did God show me as I read this week

_____

_____

_____

_____

2) Where is my love for God strong right now

_____

_____

_____

_____

3) Where is my love divided or distracted

_____

_____

_____

_____

4) One obstacle that keeps me from loving God with all my heart

_____

_____

_____

5) One concrete step I will take this week

Example: Set time for prayer, a verse to carry, a choice I will make for God first.

_____

_____

_____

_____

6) My simple rule of life for this week

Morning.
_____

Midday.
_____

Evening.
_____

7) Scripture to memorize

Write the verse and keep it with you.

_____

_____

_____

_____

8) Gratitude to warm my love for God

List three gifts from the last day.

1. _____

_____

2. _____

_____

3. _____

_____

9) Love in action

Who will I serve or encourage because I love God?

Name.
_____

Plan.
_____

_____

10) Prayer of offering

Write a short prayer to give God first place.

_____

_____

_____

_____

11) Talk with someone

Whom will I tell about my step this week?

Name.
_____

When we will talk.
_____?

12) End of week examen

Where did I love God with all my heart this week?

_____

_____

Where did I resist and what will I do next?

_____

_____

What help do I need from God and from others?

_____

_____

Week 7. Listening to Scripture with mind and heart

Focus

Receive the Bible as God's word and let it train your thoughts and habits.

Joshua 1:8 (KJV)

"This book of the law shall not depart out of thy mouth; but thou shalt meditate therein day and night, that thou mayest observe to do according to all that is written therein: for then thou shalt make thy way prosperous, and then thou shalt have good success."

2 Timothy 3:16 to 17 (KJV)

"All scripture is given by inspiration of God, and is profitable for doctrine, for reproof, for correction, for instruction in righteousness: That the man of God may be perfect, throughly furnished unto all good works."

What the verses say

Scripture is breathed out by God. Because of that, it carries authority and life. Paul names its uses. It teaches truth, exposes error, corrects our steps, and trains us in a way of living that fits God's character. The aim is not head knowledge alone but a life made ready for every good work.

Joshua hears a simple pattern. Do not let the word drift far from your mouth. Meditate on it day and night. The result is practical. You learn to do what God says. The promise is not instant ease but a wise, steady path that God calls success.

Meditation here is active. It means to read slowly, to rehearse the words, to let them turn over in the mind, and to aim for obedience. The Bible is not a book to conquer. It is a voice to receive, a light to walk by, and a seed that grows over time.

When you begin, some passages will be clear and others hard. Keep going. The goal is not to master the book but to let the book master you with grace and truth?

How to practice this on your own

Choose a simple plan. Read one Gospel slowly for a few weeks. Or read one psalm a day. Keep it small enough that you can keep it.

Use three steps. Read. Reflect. Respond. Read the passage aloud. Reflect by asking, What does this show about God and what does this call me to do. Respond with a brief prayer and one small action you will take today.

Mark one verse to carry. Write it on a card or in your phone. Say it morning and evening. Let it shape your choices.

When a passage is confusing, note your question and keep reading. Often clarity grows with time. Use a reliable Bible dictionary or notes later if you wish, but do not let confusion stop practice today?

Reflect and Practice

Key Scriptures to copy by hand

Write one or both verses on the lines below.

_____

_____

_____

_____

1) What did God show me as I read this week

_____

_____

_____

_____

2) Where is my love for God strong right now

_____

_____

_____

_____

3) Where is my love divided or distracted

_____

_____

_____

_____

4) One obstacle that keeps me from loving God with all my heart

_____

_____

_____

_____

5) One concrete step I will take this week

Example: Set time for prayer, a verse to carry, a choice I will make for God first.

_____

_____

_____

_____

6) My simple rule of life for this week

Morning.

_____

Midday.
_____

Evening.
_____

7) Scripture to memorize

Write the verse and keep it with you.

_____

_____

_____

_____

8) Gratitude to warm my love for God

List three gifts from the last day.

1. _____

_____

2. _____

_____

3. _____

_____

9) Love in action

Who will I serve or encourage because I love God?

Name.
_____

Plan.
_____

10) Prayer of offering

Write a short prayer to give God first place.

_____

_____

_____

_____

11) Talk with someone

Whom will I tell about my step this week?

Name.
_____

When we will talk.
_____?

12) End of week examen

Where did I love God with all my heart this week?

_____

_____

Where did I resist and what will I do next?

_____

_____

What help do I need from God and from others?

_____

_____

Week 8. Repentance and confession

Focus

Turn from sin and turn to God with honest words and a willing heart.

1 John 1:9 (KJV)

"If we confess our sins, he is faithful and just to forgive us our sins, and to cleanse us from all unrighteousness."

Psalm 51:10 (KJV)

"Create in me a clean heart, O God; and renew a right spirit within me."

What the verses say

Confession is agreement with God about our sin. John says God is faithful and just to forgive and to cleanse. Forgiveness is not earned by long speeches or punished delay. It rests on God's character and on the work of Christ.

Psalm 51 shows the tone of real repentance. It asks for a clean heart and a steadfast spirit. Repentance is a turning. You do not merely feel sorry. You turn from sin and toward God with trust.

Repentance is not a one time doorway only. It is also a daily path. As we walk with God we keep short accounts. We turn quickly when we see what is wrong and we accept grace that makes us new.

Honest confession brings freedom. Hiding keeps us stuck. Light heals. God's aim is restoration and growth, not shame.

How to practice this on your own

Keep a short examen at day's end. Ask three questions. Where did I love God today. Where did I resist. What help do I need for tomorrow. Speak plainly to God and receive mercy.

Name your sin without excuses. If you lied, say lied. If you were harsh, say harsh. Ask forgiveness and ask for a changed heart.

Plan one repair if needed. A text, a call, or a small act of restitution can turn confession into peacemaking. Do what is wise and safe.

Memorize a mercy verse. Keep 1 John 1:9 close. When accusation whispers, answer with the promise and step forward in newness.

Reflect and Practice

Key Scriptures to copy by hand

Write one or both verses on the lines below.

_____

_____

_____

_____

1) What did God show me as I read this week

_____

_____

_____

2) Where is my love for God strong right now

_____

_____

_____

_____

3) Where is my love divided or distracted

_____

_____

_____

_____

4) One obstacle that keeps me from loving God with all my heart

_____

_____

_____

_____

5) One concrete step I will take this week

Example: Set time for prayer, a verse to carry, a choice I will make for God first.

_____

_____

_____

_____

6) My simple rule of life for this week

Morning.

_____

Midday.

_____

Evening.

_____

7) Scripture to memorize

Write the verse and keep it with you.

_____

_____

_____

_____

8) Gratitude to warm my love for God

List three gifts from the last day.

1. _____

_____

2. _____

_____

3. _____

_____

9) Love in action

Who will I serve or encourage because I love God?

Name.

_____

Plan.

_____

_____

10) Prayer of offering

Write a short prayer to give God first place.

_____

_____

_____

_____

11) Talk with someone

Whom will I tell about my step this week?

Name.

_____

When we will talk.

_____?

12) End of week examen

Where did I love God with all my heart this week?

_____

_____

Where did I resist and what will I do next?

_____

_____

What help do I need from God and from others?

_____

_____

Week 9. Gratitude and thanksgiving

Focus

Give thanks in everything and let gratitude warm your love for God.

1 Thessalonians 5:16 to 18 (KJV)

"Rejoice evermore. Pray without ceasing. In every thing give thanks: for this is the will of God in Christ Jesus concerning you."

Psalm 103:1 to 2 (KJV)

"Bless the LORD, O my soul: and all that is within me, bless his holy name. Bless the LORD, O my soul, and forget not all his benefits:"

What the verses say

Gratitude is not denial of hardship. It is a way of seeing the world that remembers God's gifts in the middle of real life. Paul links joy, constant prayer, and thanks as God's will for us in Christ.

Psalm 103 talks to the soul. It calls memory to attention. Forget not all his benefits. Gratitude lists both the small and the great. Daily bread. Forgiven sin. Strength for a task. Hope beyond the grave.

Giving thanks in everything does not mean calling evil good. It means that even in sorrow there are gifts to notice and promises to remember. Thanksgiving keeps the heart soft and open to God.

Over time, gratitude trains desire. It turns the heart from envy and complaint toward worship and trust.

How to practice this on your own

Keep a daily thanks list. Write three specific gifts each day. Use names and details. Review the list at the end of the week.

Link thanks to ordinary moments. Thank God before you open your messages. Thank him when you cross a threshold. Thank him when you finish a task. Small thanks multiply.

Say thank you to people quickly. Write a brief note or send a message. Gratitude to others reinforces gratitude to God.

In hard weeks, practice stubborn thanks. Name one mercy you can still see. Whisper it to God and ask for strength to see another.

Reflect and Practice

Key Scriptures to copy by hand

Write one or both verses on the lines below.

_____

_____

_____

_____

1) What did God show me as I read this week

_____

_____

_____

_____

2) Where is my love for God strong right now

_____

_____

_____

_____

3) Where is my love divided or distracted

_____

_____

_____

_____

4) One obstacle that keeps me from loving God with all my heart

_____

_____

_____

_____

5) One concrete step I will take this week

Example: Set time for prayer, a verse to carry, a choice I will make for God first.

_____

_____

_____

_____

6) My simple rule of life for this week

Morning.

_____

Midday.

_____

Evening.

_____

7) Scripture to memorize

Write the verse and keep it with you.

_____

_____

_____

_____

8) Gratitude to warm my love for God

List three gifts from the last day.

1. _____

_____

2. _____

_____

3. _____

_____

9) Love in action

Who will I serve or encourage because I love God?

Name.

_____

Plan.

_____

_____

10) Prayer of offering

Write a short prayer to give God first place.

_____

_____

_____

_____

11) Talk with someone

Whom will I tell about my step this week?

Name.

_____

When we will talk.

_____?

12) End of week examen

Where did I love God with all my heart this week?

_____

_____

Where did I resist and what will I do next?

_____

_____

What help do I need from God and from others?

_____

_____

Week 10. Forgiveness given and received

Focus

Receive God's forgiveness and extend forgiveness to others with wisdom.

Ephesians 4:32 (KJV)

"And be ye kind one to another, tenderhearted, forgiving one another, even as God for Christ's sake hath forgiven you."

Matthew 6:14 to 15 (KJV)

"For if ye forgive men their trespasses, your heavenly Father will also forgive you: But if ye forgive not men their trespasses, neither will your Father forgive your trespasses."

What the verses say

Kindness and tenderheartedness spring from the forgiveness we have received in Christ. We forgive as forgiven people. Jesus teaches that an unforgiving heart contradicts the grace we depend on.

Forgiveness does not deny real harm. It names the wrong and releases personal revenge into God's hands. It may include boundaries and wisdom, especially where trust has been broken or danger exists.

Forgiveness is often a process. The decision to forgive can be made today. The feelings may follow slowly. We can keep offering the choice to God as often as the pain returns.

How to practice this on your own

Receive forgiveness first. Bring your own sins to God and rest in his mercy. People who know they are forgiven find strength to forgive.

Write a forgiveness prayer. "Father, you have forgiven me in Christ. I choose to forgive ___ for ___. I release revenge to you. Show me wise boundaries and a clean heart."

Practice small reconciliations. Answer messages you avoid. Admit your fault without excuses. Ask, "How can I make this right." Keep safety and wisdom in view.

When memories return, repeat the prayer and choose blessing instead of rehearsing injury. Replace bitter rehearsals with intercession for the person's good?

Reflect and Practice

Key Scriptures to copy by hand

Write one or both verses on the lines below.

_____

_____

_____

_____

1) What did God show me as I read this week

_____

_____

_____

_____

2) Where is my love for God strong right now

_____

_____

_____

3) Where is my love divided or distracted

4) One obstacle that keeps me from loving God with all my heart

5) One concrete step I will take this week

Example: Set time for prayer, a verse to carry, a choice I will make for God first.

6) My simple rule of life for this week

Morning.

Midday.

Evening.

_____

7) Scripture to memorize

Write the verse and keep it with you.

_____

_____

_____

8) Gratitude to warm my love for God

List three gifts from the last day.

1. _____

_____

2. _____

_____

3. _____

_____

9) Love in action

Who will I serve or encourage because I love God?

Name.

_____

Plan.

_____

_____

10) Prayer of offering

Write a short prayer to give God first place.

_____

_____

_____

_____

11) Talk with someone

Whom will I tell about my step this week?

Name.
_____

When we will talk.
_____?

12) End of week examen

Where did I love God with all my heart this week?

_____

_____

Where did I resist and what will I do next?

_____

_____

What help do I need from God and from others?

_____

_____

Week 11. Mercy and simple service

Focus

Do justly, love mercy, and walk humbly with God by serving people in need.

Micah 6:8 (KJV)

"He hath shewed thee, O man, what is good; and what doth the LORD require of thee, but to do justly, and to love mercy, and to walk humbly with thy God?"

Proverbs 19:17 (KJV)

"He that hath pity upon the poor lendeth unto the LORD; and that which he hath given will he pay him again."

What the verses say

God's requirement is plain. Justice that acts fairly. Mercy that moves with compassion. Humility that walks with God. These are not theoretical virtues. They are choices made in real relationships.

Proverbs adds a promise. To show pity to the poor is to lend to the Lord. God takes acts of mercy personally. He sees and repays in his way and time.

Mercy does not mean rescuing beyond wisdom. It means doing the good you can with what you have, without enabling harm. Justice means telling the truth and acting fairly, even when it costs.

Humble walking keeps service from pride. We remember that we also depend on mercy. We serve as people who have been helped by God.

How to practice this on your own

Choose one small, steady act. Check on a neighbor. Share a meal. Offer a ride. Keep a small bill or gift card ready for a need. Consistency matters more than impressive scale.

Practice wise generosity. Give in ways that truly help. When in doubt, ask, "What would be most useful to you right now." Sometimes listening is the first gift.

Learn to say a firm no when help would enable harm. Mercy and wisdom belong together. You can be kind and clear at the same time.

Add hidden acts of kindness to your week. Do one good thing no one knows about. Let God's smile be enough.

Reflect and Practice

Key Scriptures to copy by hand

Write one or both verses on the lines below.

_____

_____

_____

_____

1) What did God show me as I read this week

_____

_____

_____

2) Where is my love for God strong right now

_____

_____

_____

_____

3) Where is my love divided or distracted

_____

_____

_____

_____

4) One obstacle that keeps me from loving God with all my heart

_____

_____

_____

_____

5) One concrete step I will take this week

Example: Set time for prayer, a verse to carry, a choice I will make for God first.

_____

_____

_____

_____

6) My simple rule of life for this week

Morning.

_____

Midday.
_____

Evening.
_____

7) Scripture to memorize

Write the verse and keep it with you.

_____

_____

_____

_____

8) Gratitude to warm my love for God

List three gifts from the last day.

1. _____

_____

2. _____

_____

3. _____

_____

9) Love in action

Who will I serve or encourage because I love God?

Name.
_____

Plan.
_____

_____

10) Prayer of offering

Write a short prayer to give God first place.

_____

_____

_____

_____

11) Talk with someone

Whom will I tell about my step this week?

Name.
_____

When we will talk.
_____?

12) End of week examen

Where did I love God with all my heart this week?

_____

_____

Where did I resist and what will I do next?

_____

_____

What help do I need from God and from others?

_____

_____

Week 12. Integrity and truthful speech

Focus

Let your words build others up and keep your life true in public and private.

Ephesians 4:29 (KJV)

"Let no corrupt communication proceed out of your mouth, but that which is good to the use of edifying, that it may minister grace unto the hearers."

Proverbs 12:22 (KJV)

"Lying lips are abomination to the LORD: but they that deal truly are his delight."

What the verses say

Words are powerful. Paul forbids rotten speech and commands words that build up and deliver grace. Speech is not neutral. It either tears down or strengthens.

Proverbs shows God's heart. He hates lies and delights in truth. Integrity is the same person in private as in public. God's people are to be trustworthy.

Truthful speech does not mean saying everything you think. It means speaking truth in love, with timing and tone that seek the other person's good.

Integrity grows where confession is normal. When you misspeak, correct yourself. When you promise, keep it or make it right.

How to practice this on your own

Set a guard over your mouth. When anger flares, delay your reply. Breathe and pray one line, "Keep my mouth, O Lord." Then answer with clarity and restraint.

Choose three building phrases to use this week. "I was wrong." "Thank you for…" "How can I help." Use them daily.

Audit your words for a day. In the evening, list times your speech gave grace and times it did not. Plan one change for tomorrow.

Keep promises small and specific. Do not say yes lightly. When you say yes, do it promptly. If you fail, apologize and repair.

Reflect and Practice

Key Scriptures to copy by hand

Write one or both verses on the lines below.

_____

_____

_____

_____

1) What did God show me as I read this week

_____

_____

_____

_____

2) Where is my love for God strong right now

_____

_____

_____

_____

3) Where is my love divided or distracted

_____

_____

_____

_____

4) One obstacle that keeps me from loving God with all my heart

_____

_____

_____

_____

5) One concrete step I will take this week

Example: Set time for prayer, a verse to carry, a choice I will make for God first.

_____

_____

_____

_____

6) My simple rule of life for this week

Morning.

_____

Midday.

_____

Evening.

_____

7) Scripture to memorize

Write the verse and keep it with you.

_____

_____

_____

_____

8) Gratitude to warm my love for God

List three gifts from the last day.

1. _____

_____

2. _____

_____

3. _____

_____

9) Love in action

Who will I serve or encourage because I love God?

Name.

_____

Plan.

_____

10) Prayer of offering

Write a short prayer to give God first place.

_____

_____

_____

_____

11) Talk with someone

Whom will I tell about my step this week?

Name.

_____

When we will talk.

_____?

12) End of week examen

Where did I love God with all my heart this week?

_____

_____

Where did I resist and what will I do next?

_____

_____

What help do I need from God and from others?

_____

_____

Week 13. Patience and long suffering

Focus

Wait with courage and keep doing good while you trust God to work in time.

James 5:7 to 8 (KJV)

"Be patient therefore, brethren, unto the coming of the Lord. Behold, the husbandman waiteth for the precious fruit of the earth, and hath long patience for it, until he receive the early and latter rain. Be ye also patient; stablish your hearts: for the coming of the Lord draweth nigh."

Galatians 6:9 (KJV)

"And let us not be weary in well doing: for in due season we shall reap, if we faint not."

What the verses say

James uses the farmer as a living picture. Seed is in the ground but fruit takes time. Weather and seasons are beyond our control. Patience does not mean passivity. It means steady work with a heart established in hope.

Paul adds the promise that there is a due season. Weariness tempts us to quit before the harvest. Faith keeps doing good because God is faithful even when results are slow or hidden.

Patience is love stretched across time. It refuses panic. It stays with a worthy task. It bears with imperfect people and imperfect days without giving up on the good that God is growing.

How to practice this on your own

Name one area where you need patience. Write what faithful work looks like this week. Choose one small step you can repeat and let the calendar, not your feelings, carry the practice.

Use a breath prayer when you feel rush or irritation. Inhale. "Be patient." Exhale. "Establish my heart." Repeat until your body slows and you can choose a wise response.

Create a visible tracker for one quiet good work. A check mark on a calendar for prayer, for exercise, for writing, or for learning can help you stay with the seed until fruit comes.

Reflect and Practice

Key Scriptures to copy by hand

Write one or both verses on the lines below.

_____

_____

_____

_____

1) What did God show me as I read this week

_____

_____

_____

_____

2) Where is my love for God strong right now

_____

_____

_____

_____

3) Where is my love divided or distracted

_____

_____

_____

_____

4) One obstacle that keeps me from loving God with all my heart

_____

_____

_____

_____

5) One concrete step I will take this week

Example: Set time for prayer, a verse to carry, a choice I will make for God first.

_____

_____

_____

_____

6) My simple rule of life for this week

Morning.

_____

Midday.

_____

Evening.

___

7) Scripture to memorize

Write the verse and keep it with you.

___

___

___

___

8) Gratitude to warm my love for God

List three gifts from the last day.

1. ___

___

2. ___

___

3. ___

___

9) Love in action

Who will I serve or encourage because I love God?

Name.

___

Plan.

___

___

10) Prayer of offering

Write a short prayer to give God first place.

_____

_____

_____

_____

11) Talk with someone

Whom will I tell about my step this week?

Name.

_____

When we will talk.
_____?

12) End of week examen

Where did I love God with all my heart this week?

_____

_____

Where did I resist and what will I do next?

_____

_____

What help do I need from God and from others?

_____

_____

Week 14. Waiting on the Lord with hope

Focus

Place your hope in God while you wait and let him renew your strength.

Isaiah 40:31 (KJV)

"But they that wait upon the LORD shall renew their strength; they shall mount up with wings as eagles; they shall run, and not be weary; and they shall walk, and not faint."

Psalm 27:14 (KJV)

"Wait on the LORD: be of good courage, and he shall strengthen thine heart: wait, I say, on the LORD."

What the verses say

Waiting on the Lord is an active trust. It is not empty delay. It is turning toward God with expectation. Isaiah promises renewal for those who wait. The image rises from soaring to running to walking. God gives what is needed for each stage.

The psalm teaches courage in the waiting. We do not know timing, but we do know the character of the One we wait for. Strength enters the heart as we keep our eyes on him.

Hope in Scripture is a strong word. It stands on the promises of God. While we wait, he shapes us. He grows endurance, humility, and focus.

How to practice this on your own

Write a waiting list. Name what you are waiting for. Next to each item, write one way you will seek God in the waiting. Scripture to read. Prayer to pray. Act of love to keep doing.

Practice faithful presence. Keep doing today's work with care. Wash the dish. Answer the message. Finish the task. Waiting becomes holy when we give our best to what is at hand.

Return to a hope verse each day. Say Isaiah 40:31 or Psalm 27:14 aloud. Let courage rise from promise rather than from prediction.

Reflect and Practice

Key Scriptures to copy by hand

Write one or both verses on the lines below.

_____

_____

_____

_____

1) What did God show me as I read this week

_____

_____

_____

_____

2) Where is my love for God strong right now

_____

_____

_____

_____

3) Where is my love divided or distracted

_____

_____

_____

_____

4) One obstacle that keeps me from loving God with all my heart

_____

_____

_____

5) One concrete step I will take this week

Example: Set time for prayer, a verse to carry, a choice I will make for God first.

_____

_____

_____

6) My simple rule of life for this week

Morning.

_____

Midday.

_____

Evening.

_____

7) Scripture to memorize

Write the verse and keep it with you.

_____

_____

_____

_____

8) Gratitude to warm my love for God

List three gifts from the last day.

1. _____

_____

2. _____

_____

3. _____

_____

9) Love in action

Who will I serve or encourage because I love God?

Name.

_____

Plan.

_____

_____

10) Prayer of offering

Write a short prayer to give God first place.

_____

_____

_____

_____

11) Talk with someone

Whom will I tell about my step this week?

Name.
_____

When we will talk.
_____?

12) End of week examen

Where did I love God with all my heart this week?

_____

_____

Where did I resist and what will I do next?

_____

_____

What help do I need from God and from others?

_____

_____

Week 15. Simplicity and freedom from idols

Focus

Keep your heart free from rival masters and seek God first.

1 John 5:21 (KJV)

"Little children, keep yourselves from idols. Amen."

Matthew 6:33 (KJV)

"But seek ye first the kingdom of God, and his righteousness; and all these things shall be added unto you."

What the verses say

An idol is anything that takes the trust and love that belongs to God. It may be obvious like a carved image or subtle like approval, success, or comfort. John's closing command is short and urgent. Keep yourselves from idols.

Jesus gives the positive path. Seek first the kingdom of God. Put God's rule and what is right at the center. When God is first, lesser goods return to their proper place.

Simplicity is not bare life. It is a clear life where the heart is not divided by many masters. It is freedom from the clutter of false hopes.

How to practice this on your own

Do a gentle inventory. Where do your thoughts go when your mind is free. What do you fear losing most. What would make you compromise truth. These questions reveal potential idols.

Choose one declutter. Remove one app, one subscription, or one habit that pulls your heart from God. Fill that space with a small practice of seeking first.

Set a simple budget of time and money. Give first. Save a little. Live the rest with contentment. Simplicity grows in planned choices made over time.

Reflect and Practice

Key Scriptures to copy by hand

Write one or both verses on the lines below.

_____

_____

_____

_____

1) What did God show me as I read this week

_____

_____

_____

_____

2) Where is my love for God strong right now

_____

_____

_____

_____

3) Where is my love divided or distracted

_____

_____

_____

_____

4) One obstacle that keeps me from loving God with all my heart

_____

_____

_____

_____

5) One concrete step I will take this week

Example: Set time for prayer, a verse to carry, a choice I will make for God first.

_____

_____

_____

_____

6) My simple rule of life for this week

Morning.
_____

Midday.
_____

Evening.
_____

7) Scripture to memorize

Write the verse and keep it with you.

_____

_____

_____

_____

8) Gratitude to warm my love for God

List three gifts from the last day.

1. _____

_____

2. _____

_____

3. _____

_____

9) Love in action

Who will I serve or encourage because I love God?

Name.

_____

Plan.

_____

_____

10) Prayer of offering

Write a short prayer to give God first place.

_____

_____

_____

_____

11) Talk with someone

Whom will I tell about my step this week?

Name.
_____

When we will talk.
_____?

12) End of week examen

Where did I love God with all my heart this week?

_____

_____

Where did I resist and what will I do next?

_____

_____

What help do I need from God and from others?

_____

_____

Week 16. Contentment without greed

Focus

Learn contentment in every season and refuse the love of money.

Hebrews 13:5 (KJV)

"Let your conversation be without covetousness; and be content with such things as ye have: for he hath said, I will never leave thee, nor forsake thee."

Philippians 4:11 to 13 (KJV)

"Not that I speak in respect of want: for I have learned, in whatsoever state I am, therewith to be content. I know both how to be abased, and I know how to abound: every where and in all things I am instructed both to be full and to be hungry, both to abound and to suffer need. I can do all things through Christ which strengtheneth me."

What the verses say

Scripture ties contentment to God's presence. The promise I will never leave thee answers the fear behind greed. If God is with us, we can live free from covetousness.

Paul learned contentment. It did not arrive in a moment. He practiced it in lack and in plenty. Strength to be content comes through Christ. Contentment is not apathy. It is settled trust while we work and give and plan with wisdom.

Greed narrows the heart. Contentment opens it. We become more able to enjoy what we have and more ready to share.

How to practice this on your own

Practice a gratitude audit of your stuff. Walk through your space and thank God for ten specific things you already have. Notice how thanksgiving cools craving.

Set a contentment rule. For thirty days delay new purchases by forty eight hours. During the delay, pray and review needs. Many impulses will pass.

Give something away each week. A book, a tool, a coat, or your time. Generosity is training against greed and training for joy.

Reflect and Practice

Key Scriptures to copy by hand

Write one or both verses on the lines below.

_____

_____

_____

_____

1) What did God show me as I read this week

_____

_____

_____

2) Where is my love for God strong right now

_____

_____

_____

_____

3) Where is my love divided or distracted

_____

_____

_____

_____

4) One obstacle that keeps me from loving God with all my heart

_____

_____

_____

_____

5) One concrete step I will take this week

Example: Set time for prayer, a verse to carry, a choice I will make for God first.

_____

_____

_____

_____

6) My simple rule of life for this week

Morning.

_____

Midday.

_____

Evening.

_____

7) Scripture to memorize

Write the verse and keep it with you.

_____

_____

_____

_____

8) Gratitude to warm my love for God

List three gifts from the last day.

1. _____

_____

2. _____

_____

3. _____

_____

9) Love in action

Who will I serve or encourage because I love God?

Name.

_____

Plan.

_____

_____

10) Prayer of offering

Write a short prayer to give God first place.

_____

_____

_____

_____

11) Talk with someone

Whom will I tell about my step this week?

Name.

_____

When we will talk.
_____?

12) End of week examen

Where did I love God with all my heart this week?

_____

_____

Where did I resist and what will I do next?

_____

_____

What help do I need from God and from others?

_____

_____

Week 17. Purity of heart and mind

Focus

Seek a clean heart that sees God and think on what is true and pure.

Matthew 5:8 (KJV)

"Blessed are the pure in heart: for they shall see God."

Philippians 4:8 (KJV)

"Finally, brethren, whatsoever things are true, whatsoever things are honest, whatsoever things are just, whatsoever things are pure, whatsoever things are lovely, whatsoever things are of good report; if there be any virtue, and if there be any praise, think on these things."

What the verses say

Purity of heart is single hearted devotion to God. It is not mere rule keeping. It is the inner life aligned with God's light. Jesus promises that such a heart will see God. Clarity grows as the heart is cleansed and unified.

Paul gives a filter for thought life. Fill the mind with what is true, just, pure, lovely, and praiseworthy. What we think on shapes what we desire and what we do.

This path is not grim. It is beautiful. God invites us into a cleaner inner world where joy and clarity multiply.

How to practice this on your own

Set guardrails for screens. Move devices out of the bedroom. Use filters. Limit late night scrolling. Replace one hour of screen time each day with Scripture, a walk, or conversation.

Practice thought replacement. When an unclean or untrue thought appears, name it and replace it with a verse or a true statement about God. Write a short list to keep handy.

Ask for a clean heart daily. Pray Psalm 51:10 each morning. Add one practical boundary in the area that trips you most.

Reflect and Practice

Key Scriptures to copy by hand

Write one or both verses on the lines below.

_____

_____

_____

_____

1) What did God show me as I read this week

_____

_____

_____

_____

2) Where is my love for God strong right now

_____

_____

_____

_____

3) Where is my love divided or distracted

_____

_____

_____

_____

4) One obstacle that keeps me from loving God with all my heart

_____

_____

_____

5) One concrete step I will take this week

Example: Set time for prayer, a verse to carry, a choice I will make for God first.

_____

_____

_____

_____

6) My simple rule of life for this week

Morning.

_____

Midday.

_____

Evening.

_____

7) Scripture to memorize

Write the verse and keep it with you.

_____

_____

_____

_____

8) Gratitude to warm my love for God

List three gifts from the last day.

1. _____

_____

2. _____

_____

3. _____

_____

9) Love in action

Who will I serve or encourage because I love God?

Name.

_____

Plan.

_____

_____

10) Prayer of offering

Write a short prayer to give God first place.

_____

_____

_____

_____

11) Talk with someone

Whom will I tell about my step this week?

Name.

_____

When we will talk.

_____?

12) End of week examen

Where did I love God with all my heart this week?

_____

_____

Where did I resist and what will I do next?

_____

_____

What help do I need from God and from others?

_____

_____

Week 18. Stewardship of time and resources

Focus

Use time and resources wisely as gifts from God and offer your work to him.

Ephesians 5:15 to 16 (KJV)

"See then that ye walk circumspectly, not as fools, but as wise, Redeeming the time, because the days are evil."

Proverbs 3:9 to 10 (KJV)

"Honour the LORD with thy substance, and with the firstfruits of all thine increase: So shall thy barns be filled with plenty, and thy presses shall burst out with new wine."

What the verses say

Wisdom pays attention to how life is spent. To redeem the time means to buy back minutes from waste and to use them for what matters. The days are evil means time will leak away unless we choose well.

Honoring the Lord with substance means we see all we have as his. Firstfruits is the first and best. The proverb links honoring God with a promise of his provision in his way and time.

Stewardship is not just about money. It is about attention, energy, skills, and opportunities. We manage gifts so that love can reach farther.

How to practice this on your own

Plan your next day with God. List your top three callings for tomorrow. Put first what matters most. Block time for them and protect those blocks.

Create a giving plan you can keep. Choose a percentage or a steady amount to give first each month. Start small and grow as you are able.

Practice honest work and simple rest. Begin tasks with a short prayer. End the day by reviewing how you spent time and by thanking God for any good you were able to offer.

Reflect and Practice

Key Scriptures to copy by hand

Write one or both verses on the lines below.

_____

_____

_____

_____

1) What did God show me as I read this week

_____

_____

_____

_____

2) Where is my love for God strong right now

_____

_____

_____

_____

3) Where is my love divided or distracted

_____

_____

_____

_____

4) One obstacle that keeps me from loving God with all my heart

_____

_____

_____

5) One concrete step I will take this week

Example: Set time for prayer, a verse to carry, a choice I will make for God first.

_____

_____

_____

_____

6) My simple rule of life for this week

Morning.
_____

Midday.
_____

Evening.
_____

7) Scripture to memorize

Write the verse and keep it with you.

_____

_____

_____

_____

8) Gratitude to warm my love for God

List three gifts from the last day.

1. _____

_____

2. _____

_____

3. _____

_____

9) Love in action

Who will I serve or encourage because I love God?

Name.

_____

Plan.

_____

_____

10) Prayer of offering

Write a short prayer to give God first place.

_____

_____

_____

_____

11) Talk with someone

Whom will I tell about my step this week?

Name.
_____

When we will talk.
_____?

12) End of week examen

Where did I love God with all my heart this week?

_____

_____

Where did I resist and what will I do next?

_____

_____

What help do I need from God and from others?

_____

_____

Week 19. Blessing enemies and refusing revenge

Focus

Answer hostility with blessing and leave justice in God's hands.

Romans 12:17 to 19 (KJV)

"Recompense to no man evil for evil. Provide things honest in the sight of all men. If it be possible, as much as lieth in you, live peaceably with all men. Dearly beloved, avenge not yourselves, but rather give place unto wrath: for it is written, Vengeance is mine; I will repay, saith the Lord."

Matthew 5:44 (KJV)

"But I say unto you, Love your enemies, bless them that curse you, do good to them that hate you, and pray for them which despitefully use you, and persecute you."

What the verses say

These verses forbid payback. Evil for evil keeps evil alive. Instead, we provide what is honest and aim to live peaceably where it depends on us. The call is not to be naive about harm but to refuse personal revenge.

Jesus sharpens the point. Love, bless, do good, and pray for those who wound you. This is more than restraint. It is active goodwill that mirrors the mercy of God.

Leaving vengeance with God does not erase justice. It puts justice in the right hands. We can pursue wise boundaries and legal protection where needed, while refusing the poison of personal revenge.

Blessing enemies is not feeling warm toward them. It is choosing words and actions that seek their true good before God.

How to practice this on your own

Start with prayer. Speak the person's name to God. Ask for wisdom, protection, and a clean heart. Pray one blessing that does not enable harm.

Set wise boundaries. Decide what you will and will not do. Write a sentence you can use when pressure rises. Example. I will not continue this conversation while you shout. I am willing to talk when we are calm.

Replace revenge rehearsals with intercession. When the mind replays injury, stop and ask God to work for truth, for justice, and for the person's good. Then take a small step that prevents harm or adds good.

Choose one concrete good. A respectful email, a fair refund, a refusal to slander, or a quiet act of service. Let God handle the rest.

Reflect and Practice

Key Scriptures to copy by hand

Write one or both verses on the lines below.

_____

_____

_____

_____

1) What did God show me as I read this week

_____

_____

_____

2) Where is my love for God strong right now

3) Where is my love divided or distracted

4) One obstacle that keeps me from loving God with all my heart

5) One concrete step I will take this week

Example: Set time for prayer, a verse to carry, a choice I will make for God first.

6) My simple rule of life for this week

Morning.
_____

Midday.
_____

Evening.
_____

7) Scripture to memorize

Write the verse and keep it with you.

_____

_____

_____

_____

8) Gratitude to warm my love for God

List three gifts from the last day.

1. _____

_____

2. _____

_____

3. _____

_____

9) Love in action

Who will I serve or encourage because I love God?

Name.

_____

Plan.

_____

_____

10) Prayer of offering

Write a short prayer to give God first place.

_____

_____

_____

_____

11) Talk with someone

Whom will I tell about my step this week?

Name.

_____

When we will talk.

_____?

12) End of week examen

Where did I love God with all my heart this week?

_____

_____

Where did I resist and what will I do next?

_____

_____

What help do I need from God and from others?

_____

_____

Week 20. Quick to listen and slow to speak

Focus

Practice patient listening and careful words that aim for understanding.

James 1:19 to 20 (KJV)

"Wherefore, my beloved brethren, let every man be swift to hear, slow to speak, slow to wrath: For the wrath of man worketh not the righteousness of God."

Proverbs 18:13 (KJV)

"He that answereth a matter before he heareth it, it is folly and shame unto him."

What the verses say

Scripture calls for listening speed. We are to be quick to hear and slow to speak. Anger is to be slow as well because human anger does not produce God's righteousness.

Proverbs names the danger of rushing. Answering before hearing brings folly and shame. Wisdom gathers facts, feels the weight of another person's words, and then answers.

Listening is love in practice. It treats the other person as a neighbor, not an obstacle. It steadies conflict and gives truth a chance to land.

How to practice this on your own

Use the pause. Before you answer, breathe and count to three. Ask one clarifying question. Example. What mattered most to you in what you just said.

Reflect back briefly. Say, I hear that you are worried about the deadline and you want clearer updates. Is that right. Reflection does not mean agreement. It signals respect and reduces heat.

Set a time for hard talks. If a conversation is flooded, ask for a reset. Let us take twenty minutes and return with cooler heads. Prepare a clear, short statement of your view and a request you can make respectfully.

Reduce word waste. Choose one moment each day to say less and to listen more. Track how often understanding improves.

Reflect and Practice

Key Scriptures to copy by hand

Write one or both verses on the lines below.

_____

_____

_____

_____

1) What did God show me as I read this week

_____

_____

_____

2) Where is my love for God strong right now

_____

_____

_____

3) Where is my love divided or distracted

_____

_____

_____

_____

4) One obstacle that keeps me from loving God with all my heart

_____

_____

_____

_____

5) One concrete step I will take this week

Example: Set time for prayer, a verse to carry, a choice I will make for God first.

_____

_____

_____

_____

6) My simple rule of life for this week

Morning.
_____

Midday.
_____

Evening.
_____

7) Scripture to memorize

Write the verse and keep it with you.

_____

_____

_____

_____

8) Gratitude to warm my love for God

List three gifts from the last day.

1. _____

_____

2. _____

_____

3. _____

_____

9) Love in action

Who will I serve or encourage because I love God?

Name.
_____

Plan.
_____
_____

10) Prayer of offering

Write a short prayer to give God first place.

_____

_____

_____

_____

11) Talk with someone

Whom will I tell about my step this week?

Name.
_____

When we will talk.
_____?

12) End of week examen

Where did I love God with all my heart this week?

_____

_____

Where did I resist and what will I do next?

_____

What help do I need from God and from others?

Week 21. Just and fair work and money

Focus

Honor God with honest measures, fair dealings, and wholehearted work.

Proverbs 11:1 (KJV)

"A false balance is abomination to the LORD: but a just weight is his delight."

Colossians 3:23 to 24 (KJV)

"And whatsoever ye do, do it heartily, as to the Lord, and not unto men; Knowing that of the Lord ye shall receive the reward of the inheritance: for ye serve the Lord Christ."

What the verses say

God cares about fairness in trade. A false balance cheats. A just weight delights God. Honesty is worship in the workplace and in the marketplace.

Colossians calls for wholehearted work done as service to the Lord. This keeps work from becoming a stage for pride or a place for cutting corners. God himself is the audience and the rewarder.

Together these verses connect worship with invoices, schedules, and signatures. God delights in people who are accurate, fair, and diligent.

How to practice this on your own

Audit your measures. Review one area where you could shade the numbers or stretch the truth. Clean it up today. Accuracy is an act of love.

Do unseen work well. Pick a hidden task and do it thoroughly. Let God see. This trains the heart away from eye service.

Write a fairness pledge for yourself. I will price honestly, pay on time when it depends on me, communicate delays, and correct mistakes without blame shifting. Keep it where you handle money or contracts.

If you have been unfair, repair what you can. A corrected invoice or an apology can turn a page and honor God.

Reflect and Practice

Key Scriptures to copy by hand

Write one or both verses on the lines below.

_____

_____

_____

_____

1) What did God show me as I read this week

_____

_____

_____

_____

2) Where is my love for God strong right now

_____

_____

3) Where is my love divided or distracted

4) One obstacle that keeps me from loving God with all my heart

5) One concrete step I will take this week

Example: Set time for prayer, a verse to carry, a choice I will make for God first.

6) My simple rule of life for this week

Morning.

Midday.
_____

Evening.
_____

7) Scripture to memorize

Write the verse and keep it with you.

_____

_____

_____

_____

8) Gratitude to warm my love for God

List three gifts from the last day.

1. _____

_____

2. _____

_____

3. _____

_____

9) Love in action

Who will I serve or encourage because I love God?

Name.
_____

Plan.

_____

_____

10) Prayer of offering

Write a short prayer to give God first place.

_____

_____

_____

_____

11) Talk with someone

Whom will I tell about my step this week?

Name.

_____

When we will talk.

_____?

12) End of week examen

Where did I love God with all my heart this week?

_____

_____

Where did I resist and what will I do next?

_____

_____

What help do I need from God and from others?

Week 22. Encouragement that builds others up

Focus

Use words and actions that strengthen tired hearts and guide people toward good.

1 Thessalonians 5:11 (KJV)

"Wherefore comfort yourselves together, and edify one another, even as also ye do."

Proverbs 12:25 (KJV)

"Heaviness in the heart of man maketh it stoop: but a good word maketh it glad."

What the verses say

Encouragement comforts and builds. It does more than cheer. It aims at strengthening a person to keep going in what is good. A good word can lift a stooping heart.

Scripture assumes that people carry heavy loads. Encouragement is part of how God cares for his people. Words that are timely, truthful, and kind become a channel of grace.

Encouragement is not flattery. It names what is real and points toward what is right.

How to practice this on your own

Keep a short list of people to encourage. Each day choose one name. Send a sentence that is specific and kind. Example. I noticed how carefully you handled that problem. Thank you.

Use the rule of three. For every correction you must give, plan at least three sincere affirmations you can also give over the week. This keeps your influence balanced and life giving.

Let Scripture shape your encouragement. Share a verse that fits the situation and add one sentence of your own.

Practice silent encouragement too. Pray for the person by name and ask God to give strength, wisdom, and peace.

Reflect and Practice

Key Scriptures to copy by hand

Write one or both verses on the lines below.

_____

_____

_____

_____

1) What did God show me as I read this week

_____

_____

_____

_____

2) Where is my love for God strong right now

_____

_____

_____

_____

3) Where is my love divided or distracted

_____

_____

_____

_____

4) One obstacle that keeps me from loving God with all my heart

_____

_____

_____

_____

5) One concrete step I will take this week

Example: Set time for prayer, a verse to carry, a choice I will make for God first.

_____

_____

_____

_____

6) My simple rule of life for this week

Morning.

_____

Midday.

_____

Evening.

_____

7) Scripture to memorize

Write the verse and keep it with you.

_____

_____

_____

_____

8) Gratitude to warm my love for God

List three gifts from the last day.

1. _____

_____

2. _____

_____

3. _____

_____

9) Love in action

Who will I serve or encourage because I love God?

Name.

_____

Plan.

_____

_____

10) Prayer of offering

Write a short prayer to give God first place.

_____

_____

_____

_____

11) Talk with someone

Whom will I tell about my step this week?

Name.
_____

When we will talk.
_____?

12) End of week examen

Where did I love God with all my heart this week?

_____

_____

Where did I resist and what will I do next?

_____

_____

What help do I need from God and from others?

_____

_____

Week 23. Refusing grumbling and gossip

Focus

Do all things without complaint and starve gossip so peace can grow.

Philippians 2:14 (KJV)

"Do all things without murmurings and disputings."

Proverbs 26:20 (KJV)

"Where no wood is, there the fire goeth out: so where there is no talebearer, the strife ceaseth."

What the verses say

God commands a spirit that works without constant complaint. Murmuring erodes trust and poisons effort. Disputing over everything wastes energy that could be used to do good.

Proverbs uses a fire image. Gossip is fuel for conflict. Remove the fuel and the fire dies. Silence can be an act of peacemaking.

Refusing gossip does not mean ignoring wrongdoing. It means we choose right channels and honest, needed conversations rather than whispers that harm.

How to practice this on your own

Set a no complaint window each day. For one hour do your tasks with a quiet mouth. If a complaint rises, turn it into a request or a plan.

Use a stop line for gossip. I do not think it is helpful for me to talk about them. Let us discuss the issue with the right person.

If you have gossiped, repair it. Admit it to the person you spoke with and choose a better path. Replace gossip with prayer and with direct, respectful communication.

Celebrate progress. Write one sentence each evening about a moment you chose peace over murmuring or gossip.

Reflect and Practice

Key Scriptures to copy by hand

Write one or both verses on the lines below.

_____

_____

_____

_____

1) What did God show me as I read this week

_____

_____

_____

_____

2) Where is my love for God strong right now

_____

_____

_____

_____

3) Where is my love divided or distracted

_____

_____

_____

_____

4) One obstacle that keeps me from loving God with all my heart

_____

_____

_____

_____

5) One concrete step I will take this week

Example: Set time for prayer, a verse to carry, a choice I will make for God first.

_____

_____

_____

_____

6) My simple rule of life for this week

Morning.
_____

Midday.
_____

Evening.
_____

7) Scripture to memorize

Write the verse and keep it with you.

_____

_____

_____

_____

8) Gratitude to warm my love for God

List three gifts from the last day.

1. _____

_____

2. _____

_____

3. _____

_____

9) Love in action

Who will I serve or encourage because I love God?

Name.

_____

Plan.

_____

_____

10) Prayer of offering

Write a short prayer to give God first place.

_____

_____

_____

_____

11) Talk with someone

Whom will I tell about my step this week?

Name.
_____

When we will talk.
_____?

12) End of week examen

Where did I love God with all my heart this week?

_____

_____

Where did I resist and what will I do next?

_____

_____

What help do I need from God and from others?

_____

_____

Week 24. Intercession for others in prayer

Focus

Pray for people by name and carry their needs to God with steady love.

1 Timothy 2:1 (KJV)

"I exhort therefore, that, first of all, supplications, prayers, intercessions, and giving of thanks, be made for all men."

Job 42:10 (KJV)

"And the LORD turned the captivity of Job, when he prayed for his friends: also the LORD gave Job twice as much as he had before."

What the verses say

Intercession is part of God's will for our prayers. We bring others before him with requests and thanks. This widens our hearts beyond our own needs and aligns us with God's care for the world.

Job's story shows the humility and blessing that can come when we pray for others. God met him in his praying. Intercession often changes the intercessor as well as the situation.

Praying for all people does not mean praying for everyone at once. It means our prayers reach beyond our small circle and cover the kinds of people God cares for.

How to practice this on your own

Make a simple prayer grid. Five days. Five categories. Family, friends, leaders, those in trouble, those who do not know Christ. Write one or two names under each and rotate through the week.

Pray Scripture for people. Choose a short verse and insert their name. Example. Lord, let Maria be strong and of a good courage.

Pair prayer with one act of care. Send a message, share a meal, help with a task, or give a small gift card. Let love put hands and feet to your prayers.

Keep a list of answers. When you see a change or a mercy, write it down. Return thanks to God and let your faith grow for the next prayer.

Reflect and Practice

Key Scriptures to copy by hand

Write one or both verses on the lines below.

_____

_____

_____

_____

1) What did God show me as I read this week

_____

_____

_____

_____

2) Where is my love for God strong right now

_____

_____

_____

3) Where is my love divided or distracted

_____

_____

_____

4) One obstacle that keeps me from loving God with all my heart

_____

_____

_____

5) One concrete step I will take this week

Example: Set time for prayer, a verse to carry, a choice I will make for God first.

_____

_____

_____

6) My simple rule of life for this week

Morning.

_____

Midday.
_____

Evening.
_____

7) Scripture to memorize

Write the verse and keep it with you.

_____

_____

_____

_____

8) Gratitude to warm my love for God

List three gifts from the last day.

1. _____

_____

2. _____

_____

3. _____

_____

9) Love in action

Who will I serve or encourage because I love God?

Name.
_____

Plan.

_____

_____

10) Prayer of offering

Write a short prayer to give God first place.

_____

_____

_____

_____

11) Talk with someone

Whom will I tell about my step this week?

Name.

_____

When we will talk.

_____?

12) End of week examen

Where did I love God with all my heart this week?

_____

_____

Where did I resist and what will I do next?

_____

_____

What help do I need from God and from others?

Week 25. Cheerful giving and first steps in generosity

Focus

Give freely from the heart and trust God to provide as you bless others.

2 Corinthians 9:7 (KJV)

"Every man according as he purposeth in his heart, so let him give; not grudgingly, or of necessity: for God loveth a cheerful giver."

Luke 6:38 (KJV)

"Give, and it shall be given unto you; good measure, pressed down, and shaken together, and running over, shall men give into your bosom. For with the same measure that ye mete withal it shall be measured to you again."

What the verses say

Paul ties giving to the heart. We give as we purpose, not by pressure. God loves cheerful giving, which means willing and glad. The goal is not bare minimum. It is joy that participates in God's generosity.

Jesus promises that generosity has a harvest. The imagery is abundant. Good measure, pressed down, shaken together, running over. This is not a scheme to get rich. It is confidence that God cares for givers and often multiplies resources to bless more people.

Generosity is a form of trust. When you give you release control and declare that God is your provider. Over time cheerful giving frees the heart from fear and from greed.

How to practice this on your own

Choose a steady amount you can keep. Start with something small and regular. Give on the same day each month so that generosity becomes a habit.

Add one spontaneous gift each week. A small card, a meal, a ride, a few dollars, a shared tool. Ask, Who can I bless today. Then act.

Keep a giving list. Note where you give and why. Celebrate what God allows you to do. When income changes, adjust the plan with prayer.

Pair giving with prayer. Speak a blessing over the person or cause. Ask God to use the gift for real good.

Reflect and Practice

Key Scriptures to copy by hand

Write one or both verses on the lines below.

_____

_____

_____

_____

1) What did God show me as I read this week

_____

_____

_____

_____

2) Where is my love for God strong right now

_____

_____

_____

_____

3) Where is my love divided or distracted

_____

_____

_____

_____

4) One obstacle that keeps me from loving God with all my heart

_____

_____

_____

_____

5) One concrete step I will take this week

Example: Set time for prayer, a verse to carry, a choice I will make for God first.

_____

_____

_____

_____

6) My simple rule of life for this week

Morning.

_____

Midday.

_____

Evening.

_____

7) Scripture to memorize

Write the verse and keep it with you.

_____

_____

_____

_____

8) Gratitude to warm my love for God

List three gifts from the last day.

1. _____

_____

2. _____

_____

3. _____

_____

9) Love in action

Who will I serve or encourage because I love God?

Name.

_____

Plan.

_____

_____

10) Prayer of offering

Write a short prayer to give God first place.

_____

_____

_____

11) Talk with someone

Whom will I tell about my step this week?

Name.

_____

When we will talk.

_____?

12) End of week examen

Where did I love God with all my heart this week?

_____

_____

Where did I resist and what will I do next?

_____

_____

What help do I need from God and from others?

_____

Week 26. Integrity in secret places

Focus

Do what is right when no one sees and let God be your reward.

Matthew 6:3 to 4 (KJV)

"But when thou doest alms, let not thy left hand know what thy right hand doeth: That thine alms may be in secret: and thy Father which seeth in secret himself shall reward thee openly."

Luke 16:10 (KJV)

"He that is faithful in that which is least is faithful also in much: and he that is unjust in the least is unjust also in much."

What the verses say

Jesus directs our giving into the secret place, away from applause. The Father sees in secret and rewards as he chooses. Integrity is not for display. It is devotion that aims at God.

Faithfulness grows in small places. The way we handle little things reveals our true character. God trains us in the least so we can be trusted with more.

Secret integrity protects the soul. It keeps pride from swelling and keeps motives clean. Over time this hidden practice makes public life steady and trustworthy.

How to practice this on your own

Do one good work no one knows about. Clean a shared space, fix a small problem, or send an anonymous gift. Tell God only.

Set a private standard for honesty. Round up, not down, when measuring time or money. Keep promises that only you and God remember.

Use a simple privacy check. Would I do this the same way if a camera were on. If not, choose the faithful path.

Reflect and Practice

Key Scriptures to copy by hand

Write one or both verses on the lines below.

_____

_____

_____

_____

1) What did God show me as I read this week

_____

_____

_____

_____

2) Where is my love for God strong right now

_____

_____

_____

_____

3) Where is my love divided or distracted

_____

_____

_____

_____

4) One obstacle that keeps me from loving God with all my heart

_____

_____

_____

_____

5) One concrete step I will take this week

Example: Set time for prayer, a verse to carry, a choice I will make for God first.

_____

_____

_____

_____

6) My simple rule of life for this week

Morning.

_____

Midday.

_____

Evening.

_____

7) Scripture to memorize

Write the verse and keep it with you.

_____

_____

_____

_____

8) Gratitude to warm my love for God

List three gifts from the last day.

1. _____

_____

2. _____

_____

3. _____

_____

9) Love in action

Who will I serve or encourage because I love God?

Name.

_____

Plan.

_____

_____

10) Prayer of offering

Write a short prayer to give God first place.

_____

_____

_____

_____

11) Talk with someone

Whom will I tell about my step this week?

Name.

_____

When we will talk.

_____?

12) End of week examen

Where did I love God with all my heart this week?

_____

_____

Where did I resist and what will I do next?

_____

_____

What help do I need from God and from others?

_____

_____

Week 27. Perseverance in prayer and good works

Focus

Keep going in prayer and in steady good, even when answers are slow.

Luke 18:1 (KJV)

"And he spake a parable unto them to this end, that men ought always to pray, and not to faint;"

Colossians 4:2 (KJV)

"Continue in prayer, and watch in the same with thanksgiving;"

What the verses say

Jesus tells a parable so that we will always pray and not lose heart. Prayer is not a sprint. It is a steady walk. Fainting is the temptation to give up when time stretches longer than we hoped.

Paul adds two anchors. Continue and watch with thanksgiving. Watch means stay awake to what God is doing. Thanksgiving keeps prayer from turning into complaint. These verses call for durable faith that keeps asking and keeps serving.

Perseverance is not stubborn willpower. It is confidence in God's character. We carry needs to him and we do the good at hand while we wait.

How to practice this on your own

Choose a fixed prayer time you can keep. Set a reminder. Five minutes daily is better than one long session that disappears. Consistency grows strength.

Use a small loop. Pray, act, review. Pray about one need. Do one fitting action. Review tomorrow and repeat. This loop keeps perseverance practical.

Write a not yet list. Record requests that are waiting. Add a short note each week about any movement. Let small signs of grace fuel courage to keep going.

Reflect and Practice

Key Scriptures to copy by hand

Write one or both verses on the lines below.

_____

_____

_____

_____

1) What did God show me as I read this week

_____

_____

_____

_____

2) Where is my love for God strong right now

_____

_____

_____

_____

3) Where is my love divided or distracted

_____

_____

_____

4) One obstacle that keeps me from loving God with all my heart

_____

_____

_____

5) One concrete step I will take this week

Example: Set time for prayer, a verse to carry, a choice I will make for God first.

_____

_____

_____

6) My simple rule of life for this week

Morning.

_____

Midday.

_____

Evening.

_____

7) Scripture to memorize

Write the verse and keep it with you.

_____

_____

_____

_____

8) Gratitude to warm my love for God

List three gifts from the last day.

1. _____

_____

2. _____

_____

3. _____

_____

9) Love in action

Who will I serve or encourage because I love God?

Name.

_____

Plan.

_____

_____

10) Prayer of offering

Write a short prayer to give God first place.

_____

_____

_____

_____

11) Talk with someone

Whom will I tell about my step this week?

Name.
_____

When we will talk.
_____?

12) End of week examen

Where did I love God with all my heart this week?

_____

_____

Where did I resist and what will I do next?

_____

_____

What help do I need from God and from others?

_____

_____

Week 28. Daily cross bearing and following Jesus

Focus

Say no to self rule and follow Christ in daily choices.

Luke 9:23 (KJV)

"And he said to them all, If any man will come after me, let him deny himself, and take up his cross daily, and follow me."

Galatians 2:20 (KJV)

"I am crucified with Christ: nevertheless I live; yet not I, but Christ liveth in me: and the life which I now live in the flesh I live by the faith of the Son of God, who loved me, and gave himself for me."

What the verses say

Jesus calls every disciple to daily cross bearing. This means saying no to the old self that wants to rule and saying yes to the path of love and obedience. It is daily because every day brings choices that shape a life.

Paul describes the inner change. United with Christ, we die to the old way of living and rise to a new one. Christ lives in us. We now live by faith in the Son of God who loved us and gave himself for us.

Cross bearing is not misery for its own sake. It is love that accepts cost. We choose truth over comfort, mercy over revenge, generosity over hoarding, purity over indulgence.

How to practice this on your own

Name one self denial you will practice this week. It could be media limits, serving someone without credit, or giving up a purchase. Offer this choice to God as a quiet yes of love.

When a hard choice appears, pray one line. "Lord Jesus, I will follow you." Then do the next right thing that fits his words?

End the day with gratitude for any cross you carried in love. Write one sentence and ask for strength to follow tomorrow.

Reflect and Practice

Key Scriptures to copy by hand

Write one or both verses on the lines below.

_____

_____

_____

_____

1) What did God show me as I read this week

_____

_____

_____

_____

2) Where is my love for God strong right now

_____

_____

_____

_____

3) Where is my love divided or distracted

_____

_____

_____

_____

4) One obstacle that keeps me from loving God with all my heart

_____

_____

_____

_____

5) One concrete step I will take this week

Example: Set time for prayer, a verse to carry, a choice I will make for God first.

_____

_____

_____

_____

6) My simple rule of life for this week

Morning.

_____

Midday.

_____

Evening.

_____

7) Scripture to memorize

Write the verse and keep it with you.

_____

_____

_____

_____

8) Gratitude to warm my love for God

List three gifts from the last day.

1. _____

_____

2. _____

_____

3. _____

_____

9) Love in action

Who will I serve or encourage because I love God?

Name.

_____

Plan.

_____

_____

10) Prayer of offering

Write a short prayer to give God first place.

_____

_____

_____

_____

11) Talk with someone

Whom will I tell about my step this week?

Name.
_____

When we will talk.
_____?

12) End of week examen

Where did I love God with all my heart this week?

_____

_____

Where did I resist and what will I do next?

_____

_____

What help do I need from God and from others?

_____

_____

Week 29. Seeking refuge in God rather than in power

Focus

Trust God as your safe place instead of leaning on status, strength, or control.

Psalm 20:7 (KJV)

"Some trust in chariots, and some in horses: but we will remember the name of the LORD our God."

Proverbs 18:10 (KJV)

"The name of the LORD is a strong tower: the righteous runneth into it, and is safe."

What the verses say

Chariots and horses were symbols of power. The psalm warns against putting trust in human strength. God's people remember the Lord's name, which means his character and faithfulness.

Proverbs pictures God as a strong tower. Safety is found by running to him. Refuge is relational. We do not hide behind walls. We come to a Person who is mighty and good.

Modern chariots include money, connections, credentials, and control. These are not evil, but they are weak saviors. God alone holds the heart safe.

How to practice this on your own

Identify your chariots. Where do you reach for control first. Write the list and then write a short prayer that hands each item to God.

Practice the run. When fear rises, speak God's name and one attribute. "Lord, you are my refuge." "Father, you are faithful." Let this be your first move, not your last.

Choose one concrete act of trust. Be honest when a lie would protect you. Give when hoarding feels safer. Rest when worry tells you to work without end.

Reflect and Practice

Key Scriptures to copy by hand

Write one or both verses on the lines below.

_____

_____

_____

_____

1) What did God show me as I read this week

_____

_____

_____

_____

2) Where is my love for God strong right now

_____

_____

_____

_____

3) Where is my love divided or distracted

_____

_____

_____

4) One obstacle that keeps me from loving God with all my heart

_____

_____

_____

5) One concrete step I will take this week

Example: Set time for prayer, a verse to carry, a choice I will make for God first.

_____

_____

_____

6) My simple rule of life for this week

Morning.

_____

Midday.

_____

Evening.

_____

7) Scripture to memorize

Write the verse and keep it with you.

_____

_____

_____

_____

8) Gratitude to warm my love for God

List three gifts from the last day.

1. _____

_____

2. _____

_____

3. _____

_____

9) Love in action

Who will I serve or encourage because I love God?

Name.

_____

Plan.

_____

_____

10) Prayer of offering

Write a short prayer to give God first place.

_____

_____

_____

_____

11) Talk with someone

Whom will I tell about my step this week?

Name.

_____

When we will talk.
_____?

12) End of week examen

Where did I love God with all my heart this week?

_____

_____

Where did I resist and what will I do next?

_____

_____

What help do I need from God and from others?

_____

_____

Week 30. Righteous anger without sin

Focus

Handle anger with wisdom so that it serves love and does not harm.

Ephesians 4:26 to 27 (KJV)

"Be ye angry, and sin not: let not the sun go down upon your wrath: Neither give place to the devil."

Proverbs 16:32 (KJV)

"He that is slow to anger is better than the mighty; and he that ruleth his spirit than he that taketh a city."

What the verses say

Anger itself is not always sin. Scripture makes room for anger that aligns with God's justice. The warning is about timing and control. Do not let anger linger until it rots into wrath and opens the door to evil.

Proverbs prizes self control. Slow anger is better than physical might. Ruling the spirit is greater than taking a city. This shows the dignity of measured strength.

Righteous anger aims to protect good and to correct evil without violating love. It is firm and clean. It seeks repair, not revenge.

How to practice this on your own

Name what the anger is protecting. Is it your pride or a real good. If it is pride, repent. If it is a real good, choose a clear and measured response.

Use a three step response. Pause your mouth. Move your body. Pray one line for wisdom. Then choose one action that is both truthful and kind.

Close the day clean. Do not fall asleep rehearsing injury. If possible, send one respectful message or write a plan for tomorrow. Ask God to guard your heart and to guide your steps.

Reflect and Practice

Key Scriptures to copy by hand

Write one or both verses on the lines below.

_____

_____

_____

_____

1) What did God show me as I read this week

_____

_____

_____

_____

2) Where is my love for God strong right now

_____

_____

_____

_____

3) Where is my love divided or distracted

_____

_____

_____

_____

4) One obstacle that keeps me from loving God with all my heart

_____

_____

_____

_____

5) One concrete step I will take this week

Example: Set time for prayer, a verse to carry, a choice I will make for God first.

_____

_____

_____

_____

6) My simple rule of life for this week

Morning.

_____

Midday.

_____

Evening.

_____

7) Scripture to memorize

Write the verse and keep it with you.

_____

_____

_____

_____

8) Gratitude to warm my love for God

List three gifts from the last day.

1. _____

_____

2. _____

_____

3. _____

_____

9) Love in action

Who will I serve or encourage because I love God?

Name.
_____

Plan.
_____

_____

10) Prayer of offering

Write a short prayer to give God first place.

_____

_____

_____

___

11) Talk with someone

Whom will I tell about my step this week?

Name.
___

When we will talk.
___?

12) End of week examen

Where did I love God with all my heart this week?
___
___

Where did I resist and what will I do next?
___
___

What help do I need from God and from others?
___
___

Week 31. Care for creation as God's world

Focus

Receive the earth as God's gift and tend it with care and gratitude.

Genesis 2:15 (KJV)

"And the LORD God took the man, and put him into the garden of Eden to dress it and to keep it."

Psalm 24:1 (KJV)

"The earth is the LORD'S, and the fulness thereof; the world, and they that dwell therein."

What the verses say

Creation belongs to God. Psalm 24 says the earth is the Lord's. We do not own it in the final sense. We receive it to use and to guard.

Genesis gives a job description. Dress and keep. Cultivate what is good and protect it from harm. Stewardship is an act of love for the Maker and for neighbors who share the world.

Care for creation is not a side project. It is part of loving God and people. Wise use and grateful enjoyment both honor the Owner.

How to practice this on your own

Treat your place as a small garden. Reduce waste. Reuse what you can. Recycle when possible. Clean a patch of ground or a shared stairwell.

Choose daily habits that respect limits. Walk or carpool when you can. Use a reusable bottle. Repair before replacing. Small faithful choices add up.

Enjoy creation with thanks. Take a short walk and name five details you had not noticed. Let gratitude rise to the Giver.

Reflect and Practice

Key Scriptures to copy by hand

Write one or both verses on the lines below.

_____

_____

_____

_____

1) What did God show me as I read this week

_____

_____

_____

_____

2) Where is my love for God strong right now

_____

_____

_____

_____

3) Where is my love divided or distracted

_____

_____

_____

_____

4) One obstacle that keeps me from loving God with all my heart

_____

_____

_____

_____

5) One concrete step I will take this week

Example: Set time for prayer, a verse to carry, a choice I will make for God first.

_____

_____

_____

_____

6) My simple rule of life for this week

Morning.

_____

Midday.

_____

Evening.

_____

7) Scripture to memorize

Write the verse and keep it with you.

_____

_____

_____

_____

8) Gratitude to warm my love for God

List three gifts from the last day.

1. _____

_____

2. _____

_____

3. _____

_____

9) Love in action

Who will I serve or encourage because I love God?

Name.

_____

Plan.

_____

_____

10) Prayer of offering

Write a short prayer to give God first place.

_____

_____

_____

_____

11) Talk with someone

Whom will I tell about my step this week?

Name.

_____

When we will talk.

_____?

12) End of week examen

Where did I love God with all my heart this week?

_____

_____

Where did I resist and what will I do next?

_____

_____

What help do I need from God and from others?

_____

_____

Week 32. Impartiality and equal dignity for all

Focus

Honor every person as an image bearer and refuse favoritism.

James 2:1 (KJV)

"My brethren, have not the faith of our Lord Jesus Christ, the Lord of glory, with respect of persons."

Acts 10:34 (KJV)

"Then Peter opened his mouth, and said, Of a truth I perceive that God is no respecter of persons."

What the verses say

Respect of persons means treating people by appearance, status, or gain. James forbids this because it contradicts faith in the Lord of glory.

Peter learns that God shows no partiality. His grace crosses boundaries we draw. Every neighbor has equal worth before God.

Impartiality does not deny differences. It means we judge with truth and mercy, not with favoritism. We seek fairness in words and choices.

How to practice this on your own

Do a bias check. Notice who you avoid or dismiss. Write one step you can take to honor that person's dignity today.

Use equal tone and time. In conversations, give quiet people room and do not rush to please the powerful. Ask one sincere question and listen.

Make fair decisions. When you must choose between people, write the criteria first. Decide by the criteria, not by pressure.

Reflect and Practice

Key Scriptures to copy by hand

Write one or both verses on the lines below.

_____

_____

_____

_____

1) What did God show me as I read this week

_____

_____

_____

_____

2) Where is my love for God strong right now

_____

_____

_____

3) Where is my love divided or distracted

_____

_____

_____

4) One obstacle that keeps me from loving God with all my heart

_____

_____

_____

5) One concrete step I will take this week

Example: Set time for prayer, a verse to carry, a choice I will make for God first.

_____

_____

_____

6) My simple rule of life for this week

Morning.
_____

Midday.
_____

Evening.
_____

7) Scripture to memorize

Write the verse and keep it with you.

_____

_____

_____

_____

8) Gratitude to warm my love for God

List three gifts from the last day.

1. _____

_____

2. _____

_____

3. _____

_____

9) Love in action

Who will I serve or encourage because I love God?

Name.

_____

Plan.

_____

_____

10) Prayer of offering

Write a short prayer to give God first place.

_____

_____

_____

_____

11) Talk with someone

Whom will I tell about my step this week?

Name.

_____

When we will talk.

_____?

12) End of week examen

Where did I love God with all my heart this week?

_____

_____

Where did I resist and what will I do next?

_____

_____

What help do I need from God and from others?

_____

Week 33. Creative beauty offered as worship

Focus

Offer your creative work to God and let beauty serve truth and love.

Exodus 31:3 to 5 (KJV)

"And I have filled him with the spirit of God, in wisdom, and in understanding, and in knowledge, and in all manner of workmanship, To devise cunning works, to work in gold, and in silver, and in brass, And in cutting of stones, to set them, and in carving of timber, to work in all manner of workmanship."

Psalm 90:17 (KJV)

"And let the beauty of the LORD our God be upon us: and establish thou the work of our hands upon us; yea, the work of our hands establish thou it."

What the verses say

God fills people with skill. Creativity is not a small gift. It is a way the Spirit equips us for good work. The Bezalel story shows that craft and art can serve holy purposes.

Psalm 90 asks God to place his beauty on us and to establish the work of our hands. Beauty here is not vanity. It is the goodness and rightness of God shining through human work.

When creativity serves truth and love, it becomes worship. Whether you write, code, cook, paint, garden, or build, your work can be offered to God?

How to practice this on your own

Choose one small creative project this week. Set a modest scope. Make it as carefully as you can. Begin and end with prayer.

Let beauty serve someone. Write a short note with care, arrange a simple table, or design a clear document. Aim for usefulness and delight together.

Limit perfectionism. Offer your best within the time you have. Beauty grows with practice and humility.

Reflect and Practice

Key Scriptures to copy by hand

Write one or both verses on the lines below.

_____

_____

_____

_____

1) What did God show me as I read this week

_____

_____

_____

_____

2) Where is my love for God strong right now

_____

_____

_____

3) Where is my love divided or distracted

_____

_____

_____

4) One obstacle that keeps me from loving God with all my heart

_____

_____

_____

5) One concrete step I will take this week

Example: Set time for prayer, a verse to carry, a choice I will make for God first.

_____

_____

_____

_____

6) My simple rule of life for this week

Morning.

_____

Midday.

_____

Evening.

_____

7) Scripture to memorize

Write the verse and keep it with you.

_____

_____

_____

_____

8) Gratitude to warm my love for God

List three gifts from the last day.

1. _____

_____

2. _____

_____

3. _____

_____

9) Love in action

Who will I serve or encourage because I love God?

Name.

_____

Plan.

_____

_____

10) Prayer of offering

Write a short prayer to give God first place.

_____

_____

_____

_____

11) Talk with someone

Whom will I tell about my step this week?

Name.
_____

When we will talk.
_____?

12) End of week examen

Where did I love God with all my heart this week?

_____

_____

Where did I resist and what will I do next?

_____

_____

What help do I need from God and from others?

_____

_____

Week 34. Excellence and diligence in our work

Focus

Do your work with skill and steadiness as service to God.

Proverbs 22:29 (KJV)

"Seest thou a man diligent in his business? he shall stand before kings; he shall not stand before mean men."

Ecclesiastes 9:10 (KJV)

"Whatsoever thy hand findeth to do, do it with thy might; for there is no work, nor device, nor knowledge, nor wisdom, in the grave, whither thou goest."

What the verses say

Diligence is focused, steady effort. Scripture links diligence to opportunity. A skilled and faithful worker is useful in great places and small.

Ecclesiastes urges wholehearted effort while we have time. Work is not ultimate, but it matters. Done with the right heart, it becomes worship.

Excellence is not luxury. It is love paying attention. It delivers what it promises and cares for people through the quality of the work.

How to practice this on your own

Pick one area to raise the standard. Define what excellent looks like in two sentences. Meet that standard this week.

Use time blocks. Protect ninety minutes for deep work on what matters most. Silence notifications and finish one real task.

Close each workday with review. List what you finished, what you learned, and the next right task. Thank God for the chance to serve.

Reflect and Practice

Key Scriptures to copy by hand

Write one or both verses on the lines below.

_____

_____

_____

_____

1) What did God show me as I read this week

_____

_____

_____

_____

2) Where is my love for God strong right now

_____

_____

_____

_____

3) Where is my love divided or distracted

_____

_____

_____

4) One obstacle that keeps me from loving God with all my heart

_____

_____

_____

_____

5) One concrete step I will take this week

Example: Set time for prayer, a verse to carry, a choice I will make for God first.

_____

_____

_____

_____

6) My simple rule of life for this week

Morning.

_____

Midday.

_____

Evening.

_____

7) Scripture to memorize

Write the verse and keep it with you.

_____

_____

_____

_____

8) Gratitude to warm my love for God

List three gifts from the last day.

1. _____

_____

2. _____

_____

3. _____

_____

9) Love in action

Who will I serve or encourage because I love God?

Name.
_____

Plan.
_____

_____

10) Prayer of offering

Write a short prayer to give God first place.

_____

_____

_____

_____

11) Talk with someone

Whom will I tell about my step this week?

Name.

_____

When we will talk.
_____?

12) End of week examen

Where did I love God with all my heart this week?

_____

_____

Where did I resist and what will I do next?

_____

_____

What help do I need from God and from others?

_____

_____

Week 35. Honesty in speech and promise keeping

Focus

Speak plainly and keep your word even when it costs.

Matthew 5:37 (KJV)

"But let your communication be, Yea, yea; Nay, nay: for whatsoever is more than these cometh of evil."

Psalm 15:4 (KJV)

"In whose eyes a vile person is contemned; but he honoureth them that fear the LORD. he that sweareth to his own hurt, and changeth not."

What the verses say

Jesus calls for simple, truthful speech. Yea means yes. Nay means no. Extra layers used to hide intent belong to a world of manipulation.

Psalm 15 honors the person who keeps promises even when it hurts. Promise keeping reflects God's faithfulness and builds trust between people.

Truthful speech and steady promises are a quiet power. They make homes and workplaces safe. They witness to the God who cannot lie.

How to practice this on your own

Say yes less and mean it more. Before you agree, check your calendar and your energy. If you cannot do it, say no kindly.

When you fail, repair quickly. Admit the miss, apologize, and offer a concrete way to make it right. Integrity grows through honest repair?

Use a promise log. Write down every commitment you make. Review it daily until it is done.

Reflect and Practice

Key Scriptures to copy by hand

Write one or both verses on the lines below.

_____

_____

_____

_____

1) What did God show me as I read this week

_____

_____

_____

_____

2) Where is my love for God strong right now

_____

_____

_____

_____

3) Where is my love divided or distracted

_____

_____

_____

_____

4) One obstacle that keeps me from loving God with all my heart

_____

_____

_____

_____

5) One concrete step I will take this week

Example: Set time for prayer, a verse to carry, a choice I will make for God first.

_____

_____

_____

_____

6) My simple rule of life for this week

Morning.
_____

Midday.
_____

Evening.
_____

7) Scripture to memorize

Write the verse and keep it with you.

_____

_____

_____

_____

8) Gratitude to warm my love for God

List three gifts from the last day.

1. _____

_____

2. _____

_____

3. _____

_____

9) Love in action

Who will I serve or encourage because I love God?

Name.

_____

Plan.

_____

_____

10) Prayer of offering

Write a short prayer to give God first place.

_____

_____

_____

_____

11) Talk with someone

Whom will I tell about my step this week?

Name.

_____

When we will talk.

_____?

12) End of week examen

Where did I love God with all my heart this week?

_____

_____

Where did I resist and what will I do next?

_____

_____

What help do I need from God and from others?

_____

_____

Week 36. Hospitality to strangers and friends

Focus

Open your life with kindness and welcome people as God has welcomed you.

Hebrews 13:2 (KJV)

"Be not forgetful to entertain strangers: for thereby some have entertained angels unawares."

1 Peter 4:9 (KJV)

"Use hospitality one to another without grudging."

What the verses say

Hospitality is love in open form. It notices the outsider and makes space. Scripture ties it to kindness without grumbling.

Hebrews adds a holy surprise. God sometimes meets his people in the act of welcoming a stranger. This lifts ordinary welcome into sacred ground.

Hospitality is not a show. It is care. A clear table, a warm cup, a safe ride, or a listening ear can be holy work.

How to practice this on your own

Simplify welcome. Choose two easy meals you can make without stress. Keep a small basket ready with tea, a mug, and a clean towel for a guest.

Start small. Invite one person for coffee or a walk. Offer a seat and your attention. Ask one gentle question and listen well.

Practice mobile hospitality. Carry an extra umbrella, a spare charger, or a bottle of water to share. Look for small ways to make room for others.

Reflect and Practice

Key Scriptures to copy by hand

Write one or both verses on the lines below.

_____

_____

_____

_____

1) What did God show me as I read this week

_____

_____

_____

2) Where is my love for God strong right now

_____

_____

_____

3) Where is my love divided or distracted

_____

_____

_____

4) One obstacle that keeps me from loving God with all my heart

_____

_____

_____

5) One concrete step I will take this week

Example: Set time for prayer, a verse to carry, a choice I will make for God first.

_____

_____

_____

6) My simple rule of life for this week

Morning.
_____

Midday.
_____

Evening.
_____

7) Scripture to memorize

Write the verse and keep it with you.

_____

_____

_____

_____

8) Gratitude to warm my love for God

List three gifts from the last day.

1. _____

_____

2. _____

_____

3. _____

_____

9) Love in action

Who will I serve or encourage because I love God?

Name.
_____

Plan.
_____
_____

10) Prayer of offering

Write a short prayer to give God first place.

_____
_____
_____
_____

11) Talk with someone

Whom will I tell about my step this week?

Name.
_____

When we will talk.
_____?

12) End of week examen

Where did I love God with all my heart this week?

_____
_____

Where did I resist and what will I do next?

_____

_____

What help do I need from God and from others?

_____

_____

Week 37. Using gifts to serve others

Focus

Recognize what God has given you and use it to do real good.

1 Peter 4:10 to 11 (KJV)

"As every man hath received the gift, even so minister the same one to another, as good stewards of the manifold grace of God. If any man speak, let him speak as the oracles of God; if any man minister, let him do it as of the ability which God giveth: that God in all things may be glorified through Jesus Christ, to whom be praise and dominion for ever and ever. Amen."

Romans 12:6 to 8 (KJV)

"Having then gifts differing according to the grace that is given to us, whether prophecy, let us prophesy according to the proportion of faith; Or ministry, let us wait on our ministering: or he that teacheth, on teaching; Or he that exhorteth, on exhortation: he that giveth, let him do it with simplicity; he that ruleth, with diligence; he that sheweth mercy, with cheerfulness."

What the verses say

Scripture treats every person as gifted. Grace shows up in different ways. Some gifts speak. Some serve. Some lead. Some comfort. The point is not comparison. The point is stewardship. We use what God gives so that he is glorified and people are helped.

Gifts grow with use. They are not trophies. They are tools. As you use a gift, God often enlarges it. As you hold it back, it stays small. Romans names a wide range of service so that no one thinks only public gifts matter.

God supplies the ability. This guards against pride and despair. We do not have to be someone else. We offer what we have with faithfulness and love.

How to practice this on your own

List what you can do that helps people. Skills, experiences, and simple helps. Choose one to use this week for one person. Keep it small and real.

Notice where you feel joy and where others find help. The overlap often points to a gift. Keep a short record of what bears fruit.

Pray before you serve and after you serve. Before. Lord, use this. After. Thank you for any good you allowed me to do. This keeps the heart humble and glad.

Reflect and Practice

Key Scriptures to copy by hand

Write one or both verses on the lines below.

_____

_____

_____

_____

1) What did God show me as I read this week

_____

_____

_____

_____

2) Where is my love for God strong right now

_____

_____

_____

_____

3) Where is my love divided or distracted

_____

_____

_____

_____

4) One obstacle that keeps me from loving God with all my heart

_____

_____

_____

_____

5) One concrete step I will take this week

Example: Set time for prayer, a verse to carry, a choice I will make for God first.

_____

_____

_____

_____

6) My simple rule of life for this week

Morning.
_____

Midday.
_____

Evening.
_____

7) Scripture to memorize

Write the verse and keep it with you.

_____

_____

_____

_____

8) Gratitude to warm my love for God

List three gifts from the last day.

1. _____

_____

2. _____

_____

3. _____

9) Love in action

Who will I serve or encourage because I love God?

Name.
_____

Plan.
_____
_____

10) Prayer of offering

Write a short prayer to give God first place.

_____
_____
_____
_____

11) Talk with someone

Whom will I tell about my step this week?

Name.
_____

When we will talk.
_____?

12) End of week examen

Where did I love God with all my heart this week?

_____
_____

Where did I resist and what will I do next?

_____

_____

What help do I need from God and from others?

_____

_____

Week 38. Unity and keeping the bond of peace

Focus

Make every effort to keep peace with humility and love.

Ephesians 4:2 to 3 (KJV)

"With all lowliness and meekness, with longsuffering, forbearing one another in love; Endeavouring to keep the unity of the Spirit in the bond of peace."

Romans 12:18 (KJV)

"If it be possible, as much as lieth in you, live peaceably with all men."

What the verses say

Unity requires character. Lowliness, meekness, and patience make peace possible. Forbearing means we carry with each other. We make room for weakness and difference without surrendering truth.

Paul sets a wise limit. If it be possible. We cannot force peace. We can do what lies within us. We can refuse to add fuel. We can speak truth with a calm spirit. We can forgive and seek repair.

The bond of peace is a strong tie that we guard. It is worth effort, prayer, and honest work.

How to practice this on your own

Check your tone. Aim for lowliness rather than pride. When you write or speak, choose words that are accurate and respectful.

When conflict appears, ask three questions. What is true. What is my part. What would make for peace without hiding the truth. Then act on the answers you control?

Do one small peace act each day. Give a gentle answer. Delay a heated reply. Offer a simple apology. Peace grows through small seeds.

Reflect and Practice

Key Scriptures to copy by hand

Write one or both verses on the lines below.

_____

_____

_____

_____

1) What did God show me as I read this week

_____

_____

_____

2) Where is my love for God strong right now

_____

_____

_____

_____

3) Where is my love divided or distracted

_____

_____

_____

_____

4) One obstacle that keeps me from loving God with all my heart

_____

_____

_____

_____

5) One concrete step I will take this week

Example: Set time for prayer, a verse to carry, a choice I will make for God first.

_____

_____

_____

_____

6) My simple rule of life for this week

Morning.

_____

Midday.

_____

Evening.

_____

7) Scripture to memorize

Write the verse and keep it with you.

_____

_____

_____

_____

8) Gratitude to warm my love for God

List three gifts from the last day.

1. _____

_____

2. _____

_____

3. _____

_____

9) Love in action

Who will I serve or encourage because I love God?

Name.

_____

Plan.

_____

_____

10) Prayer of offering

Write a short prayer to give God first place.

_____

_____

_____

_____

11) Talk with someone

Whom will I tell about my step this week?

Name.

_____

When we will talk.

_____?

12) End of week examen

Where did I love God with all my heart this week?

_____

_____

Where did I resist and what will I do next?

_____

_____

What help do I need from God and from others?

_____

_____

Week 39. Humble submission to rightful authority

Focus

Honor rightful authority with a clear conscience and trust God above all.

Romans 13:1 (KJV)

"Let every soul be subject unto the higher powers. For there is no power but of God: the powers that be are ordained of God."

1 Peter 2:13 (KJV)

"Submit yourselves to every ordinance of man for the Lord's sake: whether it be to the king, as supreme;"

What the verses say

Scripture teaches respect for rightful authority. Order is a gift that restrains harm and promotes good. Submission here is not worship of power. It is an act for the Lord's sake that seeks the common good.

The Bible also shows limits. When authority commands sin, God must be obeyed rather than men. A clear conscience stays loyal to God while seeking to do right within lawful bounds.

This path trains humility. We practice patience, fairness, and prayer for those who govern, while we live honest and quiet lives.

How to practice this on your own

Keep a clean conscience. Pay what you owe. Tell the truth on forms. Follow just rules at work and in the community.

When a policy seems wrong, respond with respect. Ask questions. Appeal with clarity. Choose lawful and peaceful options?

Pray for those in authority. Ask God to give them wisdom, justice, and compassion. This softens the heart and steadies your words.

Reflect and Practice

Key Scriptures to copy by hand

Write one or both verses on the lines below.

_____

_____

_____

_____

1) What did God show me as I read this week

_____

_____

_____

_____

2) Where is my love for God strong right now

_____

_____

_____

_____

3) Where is my love divided or distracted

_____

_____

_____

4) One obstacle that keeps me from loving God with all my heart

_____

_____

_____

_____

5) One concrete step I will take this week

Example: Set time for prayer, a verse to carry, a choice I will make for God first.

_____

_____

_____

_____

6) My simple rule of life for this week

Morning.
_____

Midday.
_____

Evening.
_____

7) Scripture to memorize

Write the verse and keep it with you.

_____

_____

_____

_____

8) Gratitude to warm my love for God

List three gifts from the last day.

1. _____

_____

2. _____

_____

3. _____

_____

9) Love in action

Who will I serve or encourage because I love God?

Name.
_____

Plan.
_____

_____

10) Prayer of offering

Write a short prayer to give God first place.

_____

_____

_____

_____

11) Talk with someone

Whom will I tell about my step this week?

Name.
_____

When we will talk.
_____?

12) End of week examen

Where did I love God with all my heart this week?
_____
_____

Where did I resist and what will I do next?
_____
_____

What help do I need from God and from others?
_____
_____

Week 40. Courage to speak truth in love

Focus

Tell the truth with a brave and gentle heart that aims for real good.

Ephesians 4:15 (KJV)

"But speaking the truth in love, may grow up into him in all things, which is the head, even Christ:"

Jeremiah 1:7 to 8 (KJV)

"But the LORD said unto me, Say not, I am a child: for thou shalt go to all that I shall send thee, and whatsoever I command thee thou shalt speak. Be not afraid of their faces: for I am with thee to deliver thee, saith the LORD."

What the verses say

Truth without love can wound. Love without truth can mislead. Scripture calls for both together. As we speak this way, we grow up into Christ who is the head.

Jeremiah receives courage from God. Do not be afraid of faces. God promises his presence to those he sends. Courage does not mean absence of fear. It means obedience with God near.

Speaking truth in love aims at the other person's good and at God's honor. It chooses clear words, wise timing, and a calm spirit.

How to practice this on your own

Prepare before hard conversations. Write the truth you need to say in one or two sentences. Add one sentence of care. Pray for a steady tone.

Pick your moment. Avoid ambush. Choose a time when you and the other person can listen.

Accept outcomes with peace. You can control honesty and kindness. You cannot control reception. Keep your heart clean and keep doing good.

Reflect and Practice

Key Scriptures to copy by hand

Write one or both verses on the lines below.

_____

_____

_____

_____

1) What did God show me as I read this week

_____

_____

_____

_____

2) Where is my love for God strong right now

_____

_____

_____

_____

3) Where is my love divided or distracted

_____

_____

_____

_____

4) One obstacle that keeps me from loving God with all my heart

_____

_____

_____

_____

5) One concrete step I will take this week

Example: Set time for prayer, a verse to carry, a choice I will make for God first.

_____

_____

_____

_____

6) My simple rule of life for this week

Morning.
_____

Midday.
_____

Evening.
_____

7) Scripture to memorize

Write the verse and keep it with you.

_____

_____

_____

8) Gratitude to warm my love for God

List three gifts from the last day.

1. _____

2. _____

3. _____

9) Love in action

Who will I serve or encourage because I love God?

Name.

Plan.

10) Prayer of offering

Write a short prayer to give God first place.

11) Talk with someone

Whom will I tell about my step this week?

Name.
_____

When we will talk.
_____?

12) End of week examen

Where did I love God with all my heart this week?
_____
_____

Where did I resist and what will I do next?
_____
_____

What help do I need from God and from others?
_____
_____

Week 41. Bearing with one another in patience

Focus

Carry with imperfect people as God carries with you.

Colossians 3:12 to 13 (KJV)

"Put on therefore, as the elect of God, holy and beloved, bowels of mercies, kindness, humbleness of mind, meekness, longsuffering;

Forbearing one another, and forgiving one another, if any man have a quarrel against any: even as Christ forgave you, so also do ye."

Proverbs 19:11 (KJV)

"The discretion of a man deferreth his anger; and it is his glory to pass over a transgression."

What the verses say

The new life in Christ wears mercy, kindness, humility, meekness, and patience like clothing. Forbearing means we make room for the slow growth of others. We forgive as we have been forgiven.

Proverbs praises the wisdom that delays anger and passes over small offenses. This is not ignoring evil. It is refusing to be touchy and quick to take offense.

Patience in relationships reflects God's patience with us. It creates space where people can grow and where peace can remain.

How to practice this on your own

Choose one small offense to let go. Do not bring it up. Do not replay it. Pray blessing instead.

Use slow anger. When irritation rises, delay your reply and ask one question to understand. Often clarity cools heat.

Set wise boundaries when needed. Patience is not permission for abuse. You can be patient and firm.

Reflect and Practice

Key Scriptures to copy by hand

Write one or both verses on the lines below.

_____

_____

_____

_____

1) What did God show me as I read this week

_____

_____

_____

_____

2) Where is my love for God strong right now

_____

_____

_____

_____

3) Where is my love divided or distracted

_____

_____

_____

_____

4) One obstacle that keeps me from loving God with all my heart

_____

_____

_____

_____

5) One concrete step I will take this week

Example: Set time for prayer, a verse to carry, a choice I will make for God first.

_____

_____

_____

_____

6) My simple rule of life for this week

Morning.

_____

Midday.

_____

Evening.

_____

7) Scripture to memorize

Write the verse and keep it with you.

_____

_____

_____

_____

8) Gratitude to warm my love for God

List three gifts from the last day.

1. _____

_____

2. _____

_____

3. _____

_____

9) Love in action

Who will I serve or encourage because I love God?

Name.
_____

Plan.
_____

_____

10) Prayer of offering

Write a short prayer to give God first place.

_____

_____

_____

_____

11) Talk with someone

Whom will I tell about my step this week?

Name.
_____

When we will talk.
_____?

12) End of week examen

Where did I love God with all my heart this week?
_____
_____

Where did I resist and what will I do next?
_____
_____

What help do I need from God and from others?
_____
_____

Week 42. Gentleness and meek strength

Focus

Embrace the strength of a gentle spirit that follows Jesus.

Matthew 11:29 (KJV)

"Take my yoke upon you, and learn of me; for I am meek and lowly in heart: and ye shall find rest unto your souls."

Galatians 5:22 to 23 (KJV)

"But the fruit of the Spirit is love, joy, peace, longsuffering, gentleness, goodness, faith, Meekness, temperance: against such there is no law."

What the verses say

Jesus describes his heart as meek and lowly. To learn from him is to find rest. Gentleness is not weakness. It is strength under control that uses power to serve rather than to crush.

Gentleness and meekness are part of the Spirit's fruit. They grow as we walk with God. They fit any setting. There is no law against them.

A gentle person can confront and can protect. The difference is the tone and aim. The goal is always love and truth.

How to practice this on your own

Practice a soft answer. When a sharp word comes at you, lower your volume and slow your pace. Choose words that are true and kind.

Notice your hands and face. Relax your jaw. Unclench your fists. These small choices prepare your heart to answer with gentleness.

Ask Jesus to teach you his heart. Read Matthew 11:29 each morning this week. Invite the Spirit to grow meek strength in you.

Reflect and Practice

Key Scriptures to copy by hand

Write one or both verses on the lines below.

_____

_____

_____

1) What did God show me as I read this week

2) Where is my love for God strong right now

3) Where is my love divided or distracted

4) One obstacle that keeps me from loving God with all my heart

5) One concrete step I will take this week

Example: Set time for prayer, a verse to carry, a choice I will make for God first.

_____

_____

_____

_____

6) My simple rule of life for this week

Morning.
_____

Midday.
_____

Evening.
_____

7) Scripture to memorize

Write the verse and keep it with you.

_____

_____

_____

_____

8) Gratitude to warm my love for God

List three gifts from the last day.

1. _____

_____

2. _____

_____

3. _____

_____

9) Love in action

Who will I serve or encourage because I love God?

Name.

_____

Plan.

_____

_____

10) Prayer of offering

Write a short prayer to give God first place.

_____

_____

_____

_____

11) Talk with someone

Whom will I tell about my step this week?

Name.

_____

When we will talk.

_____?

12) End of week examen

Where did I love God with all my heart this week?

_____

_____

Where did I resist and what will I do next?

_____

_____

What help do I need from God and from others?

_____

_____

Week 43. Self control in body and mind

Focus

Let the Spirit train your desires and habits so that love can lead.

Galatians 5:22 to 23 (KJV)

"But the fruit of the Spirit is love, joy, peace, longsuffering, gentleness, goodness, faith, Meekness, temperance: against such there is no law."

Proverbs 25:28 (KJV)

"He that hath no rule over his own spirit is like a city that is broken down, and without walls."

What the verses say

Self control in Scripture is Spirit born temperance. It does not come from gritted teeth alone. It grows as we walk with God. The list in

Galatians shows that self control is part of a larger harvest that includes love and joy.

Proverbs pictures a life without self control as a city with broken walls. Vulnerable and easily invaded. Boundaries protect what is good. The goal is not a tight and joyless life. The goal is freedom to love because desires are trained.

Christian self control starts with the heart. The Spirit changes what we want. Then we practice choices that match the new desire. Over time habits become allies that keep us steady.

How to practice this on your own

Pick one arena. Words, food, spending, screens, or sexual purity. Write a small rule for one week that you can keep. Example. No screens after ten. Or, one dessert on weekends only. Or, pause and pray before every reply in a hot thread.

Use replacement, not just removal. When you take away a harmful pattern, fill the space with a good one. Replace late scrolling with a psalm and sleep. Replace mindless snacking with a walk and water.

Build guardrails. Move the phone to another room. Remove a shopping app. Set spending alerts. Choose a safe route home. Guardrails are not fear. They are wisdom that protects love.

Ask daily for the Spirit's help. Pray, Lord, grow temperance in me. Thank God for any small win. When you fail, confess quickly, reset the plan, and begin again.

Reflect and Practice

Key Scriptures to copy by hand

Write one or both verses on the lines below.

_____

_____

_____

_____

1) What did God show me as I read this week

_____

_____

_____

_____

2) Where is my love for God strong right now

_____

_____

_____

_____

3) Where is my love divided or distracted

_____

_____

_____

_____

4) One obstacle that keeps me from loving God with all my heart

_____

_____

_____

_____

5) One concrete step I will take this week

Example: Set time for prayer, a verse to carry, a choice I will make for God first.

_____

_____

_____

_____

6) My simple rule of life for this week

Morning.

_____

Midday.

_____

Evening.

_____

7) Scripture to memorize

Write the verse and keep it with you.

_____

_____

_____

_____

8) Gratitude to warm my love for God

List three gifts from the last day.

1. _____

_____

2. _____

_____

3. _____

_____

9) Love in action

Who will I serve or encourage because I love God?

Name.
_____

Plan.
_____

_____

10) Prayer of offering

Write a short prayer to give God first place.

_____

_____

_____

_____

11) Talk with someone

Whom will I tell about my step this week?

Name.
_____

When we will talk.
_____?

12) End of week examen

Where did I love God with all my heart this week?
_____
_____

Where did I resist and what will I do next?
_____
_____

What help do I need from God and from others?
_____
_____

Week 44. Teaching children the way of the Lord

Focus

Pass on God's truth to the young people in your life with simple, steady steps.

Deuteronomy 6:6 to 7 (KJV)

"And these words, which I command thee this day, shall be in thine heart: And thou shalt teach them diligently unto thy children, and shalt talk of them when thou sittest in thine house, and when thou walkest by the way, and when thou liest down, and when thou risest up."

Proverbs 22:6 (KJV)

"Train up a child in the way he should go: and when he is old, he will not depart from it."

What the verses say

God's words are to be in our hearts and on our lips in everyday life. Deuteronomy shows teaching as a rhythm woven into normal moments. Sitting, walking, lying down, rising. This is not heavy lectures. It is steady conversation about God in the middle of real life.

Proverbs points to long term formation. Training a child is a patient path. Seeds are planted that may sprout years later. The promise is a general pattern, not a formula. Faithful sowing matters. God gives the growth.

Whether you are a parent, a grandparent, an aunt or uncle, a neighbor, or a mentor, you can pass on what you are learning. Your quiet example speaks loudly.

How to practice this on your own

Choose one child to bless this week. Share a short verse and one sentence in your own words about what it means. Keep it warm and simple.

Use natural moments. At meals, in the car, during a walk, or at bedtime, ask one gentle question about God or the verse you shared. Listen more than you lecture.

Let them see you practice. Read your Bible where they can notice. Say a short prayer aloud for wisdom, kindness, or courage. Children learn what they see.

Be patient. Do not demand big responses. Celebrate small signs of interest. Keep planting good seed with love.

Reflect and Practice

Key Scriptures to copy by hand

Write one or both verses on the lines below.

_____

_____

_____

_____

1) What did God show me as I read this week

_____

_____

_____

_____

2) Where is my love for God strong right now

_____

_____

_____

_____

3) Where is my love divided or distracted

_____

_____

_____

4) One obstacle that keeps me from loving God with all my heart

_____

_____

_____

_____

5) One concrete step I will take this week

Example: Set time for prayer, a verse to carry, a choice I will make for God first.

_____

_____

_____

_____

6) My simple rule of life for this week

Morning.

_____

Midday.

_____

Evening.

_____

7) Scripture to memorize

Write the verse and keep it with you.

_____

_____

_____

_____

8) Gratitude to warm my love for God

List three gifts from the last day.

1. _____

_____

2. _____

_____

3. _____

_____

9) Love in action

Who will I serve or encourage because I love God?

Name.

_____

Plan.

_____

_____

10) Prayer of offering

Write a short prayer to give God first place.

_____

_____

_____

_____

11) Talk with someone

Whom will I tell about my step this week?

Name.

_____

When we will talk.

_____?

12) End of week examen

Where did I love God with all my heart this week?

_____

_____

Where did I resist and what will I do next?

_____

_____

What help do I need from God and from others?

_____

_____

Week 45. Remembering the poor

Focus

Keep people in need close to your heart and act for their good.

Galatians 2:10 (KJV)

"Only they would that we should remember the poor; the same which I also was forward to do."

Proverbs 14:31 (KJV)

"He that oppresseth the poor reproacheth his Maker: but he that honoureth him hath mercy on the poor."

What the verses say

Paul treats care for the poor as a core expectation, not an optional add on. To remember is to keep in mind and to act.

Proverbs ties our treatment of the poor to our view of God. Mercy to the poor honors the Maker because every person bears his image. Oppression insults him.

Remembering the poor is broad. It includes money, time, advocacy, and friendship. It resists indifference and moves toward real help.

How to practice this on your own

Set a small, steady gift for relief and development. Choose a trustworthy organization that serves wisely. Start now and review each year.

Keep one ready resource on you. A gift card, a snack bag, or a bus pass can meet a real need in the moment.

Learn and listen. Read or watch one thoughtful piece about poverty in your city or region. Let understanding shape how you give and serve.

Honor dignity. Use kind eyes and words. Ask a person's name and listen to their story when time allows.

Reflect and Practice

Key Scriptures to copy by hand

Write one or both verses on the lines below.

_____

_____

_____

_____

1) What did God show me as I read this week

_____

_____

_____

_____

2) Where is my love for God strong right now

_____

_____

_____

_____

3) Where is my love divided or distracted

_____

_____

_____

4) One obstacle that keeps me from loving God with all my heart

_____

_____

_____

_____

5) One concrete step I will take this week

Example: Set time for prayer, a verse to carry, a choice I will make for God first.

_____

_____

_____

_____

6) My simple rule of life for this week

Morning.
_____

Midday.
_____

Evening.
_____

7) Scripture to memorize

Write the verse and keep it with you.

_____

_____

_____

_____

8) Gratitude to warm my love for God

List three gifts from the last day.

1. _____

_____

2. _____

_____

3. _____

_____

9) Love in action

Who will I serve or encourage because I love God?

Name.
_____

Plan.
_____

_____

10) Prayer of offering

Write a short prayer to give God first place.

_____

_____

_____

_____

11) Talk with someone

Whom will I tell about my step this week?

Name.

_____

When we will talk.

_____?

12) End of week examen

Where did I love God with all my heart this week?

_____

_____

Where did I resist and what will I do next?

_____

_____

What help do I need from God and from others?

_____

_____

Week 46. Visiting the sick and the imprisoned

Focus

Bring the compassion of Christ to people who are isolated by illness or incarceration.

Matthew 25:36 (KJV)

"Naked, and ye clothed me: I was sick, and ye visited me: I was in prison, and ye came unto me."

Hebrews 13:3 (KJV)

"Remember them that are in bonds, as bound with them; and them which suffer adversity, as being yourselves also in the body."

What the verses say

Jesus identifies with the sick and the imprisoned. To visit them is to serve him. This lifts simple acts of presence into holy work.

Hebrews calls for compassionate memory. We remember people in bonds and in suffering as if we were there with them. This fuels prayer, letters, and wise care.

Visiting can look like many things. In person where possible, or through letters, calls, approved books, and practical help to families. The heart is to bring presence, dignity, and hope.

How to practice this on your own

Make a care list. Write the names of people who are sick, elderly, recovering, or incarcerated. Pray for them and choose one concrete way to show care this week.

Send presence. A short visit, a letter, a card, or a simple meal can carry love into hard places. Follow rules and safety where institutions are involved.

Be a steady friend. Isolation increases suffering. Small but regular contact brings courage. Mark a calendar reminder so care continues.

Reflect and Practice

Key Scriptures to copy by hand

Write one or both verses on the lines below.

_____

_____

_____

_____

1) What did God show me as I read this week

_____

_____

_____

2) Where is my love for God strong right now

_____

_____

_____

3) Where is my love divided or distracted

_____

_____

_____

_____

4) One obstacle that keeps me from loving God with all my heart

_____

_____

_____

5) One concrete step I will take this week

Example: Set time for prayer, a verse to carry, a choice I will make for God first.

_____

_____

_____

6) My simple rule of life for this week

Morning.
_____

Midday.
_____

Evening.
_____

7) Scripture to memorize

Write the verse and keep it with you.

_____

_____

_____

_____

8) Gratitude to warm my love for God

List three gifts from the last day.

1. _____

_____

2. _____

_____

3. _____

_____

9) Love in action

Who will I serve or encourage because I love God?

Name.

_____

Plan.

_____

_____

10) Prayer of offering

Write a short prayer to give God first place.

_____

_____

_____

_____

11) Talk with someone

Whom will I tell about my step this week?

Name.
_____

When we will talk.
_____?

12) End of week examen

Where did I love God with all my heart this week?
_____

_____

Where did I resist and what will I do next?
_____

_____

What help do I need from God and from others?
_____

_____

Week 47. Caring for widows and orphans

Focus

Practice pure religion by caring for those who have lost protection and support.

James 1:27 (KJV)

"Pure religion and undefiled before God and the Father is this, To visit the fatherless and widows in their affliction, and to keep himself unspotted from the world."

Psalm 68:5 (KJV)

"A father of the fatherless, and a judge of the widows, is God in his holy habitation."

What the verses say

James gives a clear picture of devotion that God values. Care for the vulnerable and a clean life before the world. Visiting means attentive presence that brings practical help.

Psalm 68 shows God's heart. He names himself a father to the fatherless and a defender of widows. When we care for them, we reflect his character.

This call applies broadly. It includes single parents, foster children, and elderly neighbors who live alone. God's people move toward those who need family strength.

How to practice this on your own

Identify one widow, widower, single parent, or foster family you know. Offer one specific help this week. A ride, a meal, a repair, or an errand.

Consider mentoring or tutoring a child who needs support. Many programs allow safe, structured involvement.

Keep yourself unspotted. As you serve, guard your own life. Practice honesty, purity, and humility so that your help is clean and steady.

Reflect and Practice

Key Scriptures to copy by hand

Write one or both verses on the lines below.

_____

_____

_____

_____

1) What did God show me as I read this week

_____

_____

_____

_____

2) Where is my love for God strong right now

_____

_____

_____

_____

3) Where is my love divided or distracted

_____

_____

_____

_____

4) One obstacle that keeps me from loving God with all my heart

_____

_____

_____

_____

5) One concrete step I will take this week

Example: Set time for prayer, a verse to carry, a choice I will make for God first.

_____

_____

_____

_____

6) My simple rule of life for this week

Morning.

_____

Midday.

_____

Evening.

_____

7) Scripture to memorize

Write the verse and keep it with you.

_____

_____

_____

_____

8) Gratitude to warm my love for God

List three gifts from the last day.

1. _____

_____

2. _____

_____

3. _____

_____

9) Love in action

Who will I serve or encourage because I love God?

Name.

_____

Plan.

_____

_____

10) Prayer of offering

Write a short prayer to give God first place.

_____

_____

_____

_____

11) Talk with someone

Whom will I tell about my step this week?

Name.

_____

When we will talk.
_____?

12) End of week examen

Where did I love God with all my heart this week?

_____

_____

Where did I resist and what will I do next?

_____

_____

What help do I need from God and from others?

_____

_____

Week 48. Courageous witness to the good news

Focus

Share your hope in Christ with clarity, humility, and love.

1 Peter 3:15 (KJV)

"But sanctify the Lord God in your hearts: and be ready always to give an answer to every man that asketh you a reason of the hope that is in you with meekness and fear:"

Romans 1:16 (KJV)

"For I am not ashamed of the gospel of Christ: for it is the power of God unto salvation to every one that believeth; to the Jew first, and also to the Greek."

What the verses say

Witness begins in the heart. We set apart Christ as Lord and then we speak from that center. Peter calls us to be ready with a reason for our hope, delivered with meekness and respectful fear.

Paul refuses shame about the gospel. It is not a weak message. It is God's power to rescue people who believe. This gives courage to speak even when responses vary.

Courageous witness is not loudness. It is clarity with love. It tells the truth about Jesus and invites trust without pressure or pride.

How to practice this on your own

Write your two minute story. Before Christ, how you met Christ, and one change since. Keep it simple and honest.

Pray daily for two people who do not yet follow Jesus. Ask for open doors and for a gentle, clear tongue.

Use questions to invite conversation. What gives you hope right now. What do you think about Jesus. Listen well and share a short piece of your story or a verse that fits.

Live a visible life. Let your good works shine so people see and ask why. Be ready to point to Christ as the source of your hope.

Reflect and Practice

Key Scriptures to copy by hand

Write one or both verses on the lines below.

_____

_____

_____

_____

1) What did God show me as I read this week

_____

_____

_____

2) Where is my love for God strong right now

_____

_____

_____

_____

3) Where is my love divided or distracted

_____

_____

_____

_____

4) One obstacle that keeps me from loving God with all my heart

_____

_____

_____

_____

5) One concrete step I will take this week

Example: Set time for prayer, a verse to carry, a choice I will make for God first.

_____

_____

_____

_____

6) My simple rule of life for this week

Morning.

_____

Midday.

_____

Evening.

_____

7) Scripture to memorize

Write the verse and keep it with you.

_____

_____

_____

_____

8) Gratitude to warm my love for God

List three gifts from the last day.

1. _____

_____

2. _____

_____

3. _____

_____

9) Love in action

Who will I serve or encourage because I love God?

Name.

_____

Plan.

_____

_____

10) Prayer of offering

Write a short prayer to give God first place.

_____

_____

_____

_____

11) Talk with someone

Whom will I tell about my step this week?

Name.

_____

When we will talk.

_____?

12) End of week examen

Where did I love God with all my heart this week?

_____

_____

Where did I resist and what will I do next?

_____

_____

What help do I need from God and from others?

_____

_____

Week 49. Sexual purity and honor

Focus

Honor God with your body and treat others with dignity and self control.

1 Thessalonians 4:3 to 5 (KJV)

"For this is the will of God, even your sanctification, that ye should abstain from fornication: That every one of you should know how to possess his vessel in sanctification and honour; Not in the lust of concupiscence, even as the Gentiles which know not God:"

1 Corinthians 6:18 to 20 (KJV)

"Flee fornication. Every sin that a man doeth is without the body; but he that committeth fornication sinneth against his own body. What? know ye not that your body is the temple of the Holy Ghost which is in you, which ye have of God, and ye are not your own? For ye are bought with a price: therefore glorify God in your body, and in your spirit, which are God's."

What the verses say

God's will includes our holiness in sexual life. Scripture calls us to abstain from sexual sin and to learn self control. Possess his vessel means to master the body with honor rather than to be mastered by passion.

Paul gives reasons for purity. Your body belongs to God. The Spirit lives in you. You were bought with a price at the cross. Sexual sin harms the body and the soul. Purity is not small minded. It is sacred minded. It protects love and keeps the heart clear.

Flee is an action word. We do not debate with temptation. We turn and move. God's commands are for our good and for the dignity of others.

How to practice this on your own

Name your danger zones. Late night scrolling, isolation, certain shows, or certain places. Write a plan to avoid or limit them. Replace them with better choices that feed life.

Build guardrails. Move devices out of the bedroom. Use filters. Keep doors open. Choose public places for dates. Decide your no before pressure appears.

Strengthen the heart. Pray Psalm 51:10 each morning. Memorize 1 Thessalonians 4:3 to 5. When temptation rises, quote the verse, step away, and take a walk.

Pursue clean affection. Learn to honor people as image bearers. Choose conversations, hobbies, and friendships that help you love with clarity and respect.

Reflect and Practice

Key Scriptures to copy by hand

Write one or both verses on the lines below.

_____

_____

_____

_____

1) What did God show me as I read this week

_____

_____

_____

_____

2) Where is my love for God strong right now

_____

_____

_____

_____

3) Where is my love divided or distracted

_____

_____

_____

_____

4) One obstacle that keeps me from loving God with all my heart

_____

_____

_____

_____

5) One concrete step I will take this week

Example: Set time for prayer, a verse to carry, a choice I will make for God first.

_____

_____

_____

_____

6) My simple rule of life for this week

Morning.

___

Midday.

___

Evening.

___

7) Scripture to memorize

Write the verse and keep it with you.

___

___

___

___

8) Gratitude to warm my love for God

List three gifts from the last day.

1. ___

___

2. ___

___

3. ___

___

9) Love in action

Who will I serve or encourage because I love God?

Name.

___

Plan.

_____

_____

10) Prayer of offering

Write a short prayer to give God first place.

_____

_____

_____

11) Talk with someone

Whom will I tell about my step this week?

Name.

_____

When we will talk.

_____?

12) End of week examen

Where did I love God with all my heart this week?

_____

_____

Where did I resist and what will I do next?

_____

_____

What help do I need from God and from others?

_____

Week 50. Hiding the word in your heart

Focus

Let Scripture dwell in you richly through meditation and memory.

Psalm 119:11 (KJV)

"Thy word have I hid in mine heart, that I might not sin against thee."

Colossians 3:16 (KJV)

"Let the word of Christ dwell in you richly in all wisdom; teaching and admonishing one another in psalms and hymns and spiritual songs, singing with grace in your hearts to the Lord."

What the verses say

To hide the word in the heart is to store it where choices are made. Scripture internalized becomes light for the path and strength against sin.

Paul calls us to let the word dwell richly. Richly suggests plenty and depth. The word fills the inner rooms. It shapes wisdom, speech, and song.

Memory is not only for scholars. It is for ordinary disciples who want God's voice near at hand in real time.

How to practice this on your own

Start a small memory plan. One verse per week. Write it on a card. Read it morning and evening. Speak it aloud and emphasize different words.

Use a memory map. Break the verse into phrases. Picture each phrase with a simple image. Link the images in order to help recall.

Review often. Old verses fade unless refreshed. Keep a short rotation. Monday review week one, Tuesday review week two, and so on.

Pray the verse. Turn it into first person prayer. This moves Scripture from lips to life.

Reflect and Practice

Key Scriptures to copy by hand

Write one or both verses on the lines below.

_____

_____

_____

_____

1) What did God show me as I read this week

_____

_____

_____

_____

2) Where is my love for God strong right now

_____

_____

_____

_____

3) Where is my love divided or distracted

_____

_____

_____

4) One obstacle that keeps me from loving God with all my heart

_____

_____

_____

5) One concrete step I will take this week

Example: Set time for prayer, a verse to carry, a choice I will make for God first.

_____

_____

_____

_____

6) My simple rule of life for this week

Morning.

_____

Midday.

_____

Evening.

_____

7) Scripture to memorize

Write the verse and keep it with you.

_____

_____

_____

_____

8) Gratitude to warm my love for God

List three gifts from the last day.

1. _____

_____

2. _____

_____

3. _____

_____

9) Love in action

Who will I serve or encourage because I love God?

Name.

_____

Plan.

_____

_____

10) Prayer of offering

Write a short prayer to give God first place.

_____

_____

_____

11) Talk with someone

Whom will I tell about my step this week?

Name.

_____

When we will talk.
_____?

12) End of week examen

Where did I love God with all my heart this week?

_____

_____

Where did I resist and what will I do next?

_____

_____

What help do I need from God and from others?

_____

_____

Week 51. Lament and hope in sorrow

Focus

Bring grief and confusion to God with honest words that end in hope.

Psalm 34:18 (KJV)

"The LORD is nigh unto them that are of a broken heart; and saveth such as be of a contrite spirit."

Psalm 42:5 (KJV)

"Why art thou cast down, O my soul? and why art thou disquieted in me? hope thou in God: for I shall yet praise him for the help of his countenance."

What the verses say

God draws near to the brokenhearted. He saves the crushed in spirit. Lament tells the truth about pain while turning toward God, not away.

Psalm 42 models a dialogue with the soul. It asks hard questions and then commands hope. I shall yet praise him. Lament is a path through grief toward trust.

Biblical lament is not grumbling. It is faithful sorrow that brings tears, questions, and waiting into God's presence.

How to practice this on your own

Write a psalm of lament in your own words. Use four moves. Address God. Bring complaint. Ask boldly. Choose to trust. Keep it simple and honest.

Create a comfort kit. A marked Bible passage, a journal, a soft blanket, a box of tissues, and a plan for a walk. When sorrow flares, pick up the kit and meet with God.

Share grief with one safe person if you can. If not, write a letter to God. Return to Psalm 34:18 and Psalm 42:5 often until hope lifts again.

Reflect and Practice

Key Scriptures to copy by hand

Write one or both verses on the lines below.

_____

_____

_____

_____

1) What did God show me as I read this week

_____

_____

_____

_____

2) Where is my love for God strong right now

_____

_____

_____

_____

3) Where is my love divided or distracted

_____

_____

_____

_____

4) One obstacle that keeps me from loving God with all my heart

_____

_____

_____

_____

5) One concrete step I will take this week

Example: Set time for prayer, a verse to carry, a choice I will make for God first.

_____

_____

_____

_____

6) My simple rule of life for this week

Morning.

_____

Midday.

_____

Evening.

_____

7) Scripture to memorize

Write the verse and keep it with you.

_____

_____

_____

_____

8) Gratitude to warm my love for God

List three gifts from the last day.

1. _____

_____

2. _____

_____

3. _____

_____

9) Love in action

Who will I serve or encourage because I love God?

Name.

_____

Plan.

_____

_____

10) Prayer of offering

Write a short prayer to give God first place.

_____

_____

_____

_____

11) Talk with someone

Whom will I tell about my step this week?

Name.

_____

When we will talk.
_____?

12) End of week examen

Where did I love God with all my heart this week?

_____

_____

Where did I resist and what will I do next?

_____

_____

What help do I need from God and from others?

_____

_____

Week 52. Living sacrifice and a renewed mind

Focus

Offer your whole life to God and let him transform your thinking.

Romans 12:1 to 2 (KJV)

"I beseech you therefore, brethren, by the mercies of God, that ye present your bodies a living sacrifice, holy, acceptable unto God, which is your reasonable service. And be not conformed to this world: but be ye transformed by the renewing of your mind, that ye may prove what is that good, and acceptable, and perfect, will of God."

Psalm 19:14 (KJV)

"Let the words of my mouth, and the meditation of my heart, be acceptable in thy sight, O LORD, my strength, and my redeemer."

What the verses say

Paul appeals to God's mercies as the reason for a whole life response. We present our bodies to God as living sacrifices. This is not a one time moment only. It is a daily offering of all we are for his will.

Transformation happens as the mind is renewed. We refuse to be pressed into the world's mold. We receive new patterns of thought that match God's truth. The result is discernment of what pleases God.

Psalm 19:14 turns the vision into prayer. We ask that mouth and heart be acceptable to God. This is a fitting final step for a year of practice.

How to practice this on your own

Begin each morning with a simple offering. Lord, I present my body and mind to you. Use my eyes, hands, words, and thoughts for what is good today.

Renew your mind with Scripture. Replace untrue stories with God's truth. When a lie appears, answer it with a verse you have memorized.

Choose one area to present in a new way. Work, rest, money, or relationships. Define one concrete choice that would please God and do it with joy.

End the week by writing what God has done this year. Thank him for any change he has begun. Ask for grace to continue in simple, steady love.

Reflect and Practice

Key Scriptures to copy by hand

Write one or both verses on the lines below.

_____

_____

_____

_____

1) What did God show me as I read this week

_____

_____

_____

_____

2) Where is my love for God strong right now

_____

_____

_____

_____

3) Where is my love divided or distracted

_____

_____

_____

_____

4) One obstacle that keeps me from loving God with all my heart

_____

_____

_____

_____

5) One concrete step I will take this week

Example: Set time for prayer, a verse to carry, a choice I will make for God first.

_____

_____

_____

_____

6) My simple rule of life for this week

Morning.
_____

Midday.
_____

Evening.
_____

7) Scripture to memorize

Write the verse and keep it with you.

_____

_____

_____

_____

8) Gratitude to warm my love for God

List three gifts from the last day.

1. _____

_____

2. _____

_____

3. _____

_____

9) Love in action

Who will I serve or encourage because I love God?

Name.
_____

Plan.
_____
_____

10) Prayer of offering

Write a short prayer to give God first place.

_____
_____
_____
_____

11) Talk with someone

Whom will I tell about my step this week?

Name.
_____

When we will talk.
_____?

12) End of week examen

Where did I love God with all my heart this week?

_____
_____

Where did I resist and what will I do next?

_____

_____

What help do I need from God and from others?

_____

_____

Afterword. Keep Walking in Love

You have spent a year practicing a simple truth. God loved you first. Every step in this book has been an answer to that love. Not a performance. Not a race. Just an honest yes to the One who calls you by name.

As you turn the final page, consider how far you have come. You began with small prayers and short passages. You learned to listen and to obey in ordinary places. You chose truth when a shortcut tempted you. You forgave when anger felt easier. You gave when saving felt safer. You waited when pushing would have done harm. None of those choices were wasted. Each was a seed. God sees in secret. He waters the ground you walk and he is patient with your growth.

Where do you go from here. Keep it simple. Keep it steady. Open your Bible tomorrow and read a few verses slowly. Ask the same two questions you asked all year. What does this show me about God. What is one small step I can take today. Write a single sentence in a notebook and then go do it. If you stumble, begin again. If you feel dry, copy a psalm by hand. If you feel grateful, sing. If you feel anxious, turn your worry into a short prayer and carry one promise in your pocket?

Let love stay practical. Keep a short list of people to bless. Choose honesty over hurry. Rest one day each week and let your heart learn that you are kept by God, not by constant motion. Put your phone down for a time each day and lift your eyes to the nearest person. Learn to say thank you more than you complain. These are not small things. They are the shape of love in the modern world.

Return to your favorite weeks when a season calls for them. If peacemaking is hard, revisit those pages and take one step. If contentment slips, read again the verses that taught you the holy art of enough. If courage fades, go back to the passages that steadied your witness. You do not need a new secret. You need the same truth in a fresh day.

You may decide to walk these fifty two weeks again. Many have found that the second time through is deeper than the first. You will recognize a line you skimmed last time and find it is now the exact word you need. God is like that. He meets you where you are and moves you forward with mercy.

Finally, remember this. The love you offer God is never lonely work. Even when you practice in a quiet room, you join a great company of saints who have read these same words and prayed these same prayers across centuries. You are part of a larger story. The One who began a good work in you will complete it. Take the next faithful step. Lift your eyes. Keep walking in love.

www.ingramcontent.com/pod-product-compliance
Lightning Source LLC
Chambersburg PA
CBHW082059230426
43670CB00017B/2891